Puerto Rico
Middle Road to Freedom

The Age of the Baroque

American Experiences in Military Government in World War II
   (*with Associates*)

Constitutional Government and Democracy

Constitutional Reason of State

Foreign Policy in the Making—The Search for a New Balance of
   Power

Inevitable Peace

The New Belief in the Common Man

The Philosophy of Hegel

The Philosophy of Kant

The Philosophy of Law in Historical Perspective

The Politica Methodice Digesta of Johannes Althusius

Responsible Bureaucracy—A Study of the Swiss Civil Service
   (*with Taylor Cole*)

Studies in Federalism (*with Robert Bowie, ed.*)

Totalitarian Dictatorship and Autocracy (*with Z. Brzezinski*)

Puerto Rico
Middle Road to Freedom

Fuero Fundamental

CARL J. FRIEDRICH

Eaton Professor of the Science of Government
Harvard University

Rinehart & Company, Inc.

Publishers, New York

Preface

THE STUDY HERE PRESENTED was delivered as the first *University Lecture* at the University of Puerto Rico in January, 1958. These University Lectures, given at the invitation of Dr. Jaime Benitez, Chancellor of the University of Puerto Rico, were established to bring to both students and the general public the findings in the social sciences, the natural sciences, and the humanities three times a year.

I want to thank my friends Professors Kenneth Galbraith and Henry Wells, who both share my deep concern for the future of this beautiful island of Puerto Rico and its gifted and generous people. They critically reviewed the text and made helpful suggestions. I have dedicated the lectures to my son Otto, because of his abiding sympathy for all the underprivileged of the world.

C.J.F.

Cambridge, Mass.
February, 1959

Contents

Puerto Rico
Middle Road to Freedom

1

Freedom with Justice

Freedom is one of the most precious gifts that the
heavens have bestowed upon men . . . the treas-
ures locked in the earth or hidden in the depths
of the sea are not to be compared with it.
Cervantes, DON QUICHOTE, II, LVIII.

THE VAST RANGE of issues which divide states, parties, and move-
ments in the world today can be reduced to the ancient argument over freedom versus justice. Everyone wants, of course,
both freedom and justice. But the "free world" puts freedom
ahead of justice, while the totalitarians put justice, social justice,
ahead of freedom. With Anatole France, they mock at the freedom of every Frenchman to sleep under the Seine bridges; freedom of speech does not include, in their view, freedom to question their program for planning social justice. This argument
is familiar to all, and even though the more ardent partisans of
each side will quarrel over specific formulations, they will settle
for some compromise along these lines. The Declaration of Fundamental Human Rights, adopted by the United Nations, was
essentially such a compromise: it embodied both positions, and
it could do so, because no sanctions were provided for carrying
the provisions of this Declaration into effect.[1]

Any attempt to discover a rational principle of preference
for either freedom or justice, once it is admitted that both are

1

basic values, presupposes a clarification of their "meaning."
What do they refer to in terms of the concrete human situations
they are supposed to affect? Clearly both of them are calls to
action. Like all values, they suggest norms or standards which,
applied to existing situations, would presumably rectify shortcomings. Clearly, both are interdependent, as is shown when
we ask: how can any order which reduces man's freedom be
just? Or: how can man be said to be truly free, if he is suffering
from injustice?

Questions of this sort have often been asked, but we must
not be afraid of their familiar ring. The human comedy continues from generation to generation, never entirely the same,
never entirely new. The novelty is visible only against the back-
drop of the familiar, the universal only discernible within the
context of the bewildering array of seemingly unique events.

Puerto Rico's unique achievement is a novel combination
of freedom and justice. It is that, because it does not fit the
familiar patterns of colonial dependence or sovereign independence, of capitalist freedom or of socialist collective justice and
planning. It goes beyond known forms of federalism, as it goes
beyond accepted notions of cultural autonomy. The confused
and confusing discussion in the United Nations over the question as to whether Puerto Rico is now a self-governing community or still a dependent territory of the United States reveals how novel the Puerto Rican state is.[2] Existing categories do
not suffice for comprehending what has happened.

In speaking of this achievement, I do not wish to suggest
that this work was accomplished by the Puerto Ricans alone. To
be sure, the people of that sunny island bore the major burden,
and their remarkable leaders can claim a large share of the credit
for having marshaled the inventive genius which brought about
the solution of their problems. But they could not have done it
without the active and devoted work of a host of other Americans—*Norteamericanos* in the island's native tongue—and more

especially of those members of Congress and of the administration who had to authorize and eventually to accept what was done in the political and constitutional sphere, and who had to provide and continue to grant the funds without which the economic development of Operation Bootstrap (Chapter II) would have been impossible. If I am right that Puerto Rico represents a unique achievement in the world of today, America as a whole can share in the pride which this achievement justifies.

But is it really a unique and novel solution of the problem of freedom versus justice? What does freedom really mean? Many ingenious answers have been given to this question. A group of researchers recently surveyed a large body of these writings in an effort to discover a common ground.[3] The results of their inquiry are summed up in the proposition that there is general agreement that freedom means "independence from something." [4] There can be no question that "independence" * is a central aspect of freedom, but first we must ask whom this "independence" refers to? For it may be the independence of the individual from social and communal bonds; it may also be the independence of one group from another. Often these two kinds of independence do not go together. Those most ardently concerned with the independence of a group, say a church or a nation, are quite ready to subordinate the members of their group completely to the group's control. These and related facts show that the conception of freedom merely as independence is not enough; it does not exhaust the meaning of freedom. Freedom is also a matter of positive direction. The contrast often drawn between "freedom from" and "freedom for" is meant to suggest this aspect of the matter, but it does not do so very clearly, the reason being that the expression

---

* It should be stated emphatically at the outset that in Puerto Rico's political history the term independence has had a specific partisan meaning, radically at variance with this use. It has meant a "sovereign republic" outside any federal union.

"freedom for" covers several aspects that ought to be distinguished.

One dimension of the so-called "freedom for" is the freedom that manifests itself in participation. Indeed, the Greeks, when talking about freedom, when calling themselves *hoi eleutheroi*, the free, were largely thinking of freedom in terms of participating in the community's life and decisions. The Greek polis knew little of the freedom that is independence; there were no bills of rights, and the life of the citizen of a typical city was not very independent.[5] But it was a life of constant participation, especially in the democratic cities, where the citizen shared not only in legislation, but in executive and judicial activity as well. At the same time, the Greeks had a very poignant sense of external freedom as independence; indeed this sense was so pronounced as to prevent them from ever achieving genuine federal union.

Looking at Puerto Rican politics with this thought in mind, we might say that the Statehood Party has been preoccupied with the freedom of participation, while the *Independentistas* have been prepared to sacrifice all to the freedom of independence. But it is a matter of participation by or independence of the people of Puerto Rico as a whole in federal decisions; when it comes to the individual Puerto Rican, their position is almost the reverse. This sharp conflict might be transcended, when a balanced combination of two kinds of freedom is achieved.

We have to recognize, then, two kinds of freedom, freedom seen as independence, and freedom seen as participation. This dual nature of freedom constituting its existential dialectic, while clearly of basic importance, still leaves us with the question of the underlying common ground. That common ground is the capacity to decide. The making of choices is a basic human experience.[6] Freedom as independence as well as freedom as participation both refer to such choices. But the focal point is different. Independent choices are choices made in the personal or private sphere, participating choices are choices made in the communal or public sphere. Where the line is to be drawn, depends upon specific aspects of the situations in which human beings find themselves. Thus if the situation is that of family life, the communal sphere is that of the family, whereas the personal sphere is that of the individual member. If the situation is that of government, the family may become largely part of the personal sphere, and part of the freedom as independence (namely freedom from government interference), whereas the communal sphere would be that of the government, and the freedom of participating therein would be maximized by extensive democratization.

It is clear from this example that the problems of group freedom are parallel to the problems of the freedom of persons. This is true on the several levels of group relations. It is exemplified in the theory and practice of federalism and international relations. In both these situations, we find autonomous communities organizing their relationships by combining and balancing the two kinds of freedom, the freedom that is independence and the freedom that provides participation.

For a fuller understanding of what this means for Puerto Rico, the problem of federalism requires further elucidation. Federalism used to be thought of largely in terms of sovereignty, and the most important issue was believed to be the contrast between a federal state and a confederation of states. Thinking still in terms of the old territorial state of monarchical antecedents, it was widely believed—and still is—that the crucial question is: where is sovereignty located in such a structure. But federalism should not be considered as a static pattern, as a fixed and precise division of powers between central and local authorities. Instead, it should be seen as the process of federalizing a political community, that is to say, as the process

by which a number of separate political organizations, be they
states or any other kind of group, enter into arrangements for
making joint decisions on shared problems. But this is not all.
Federalism is also the reverse process by which a hitherto unitary
political organization becomes decentralized to the point where
separate and distinct political communities arise and become
politically organized and capable of making their own decisions
on their own problems. This is the federalism which applies to
former colonial territories who remain bound by shared problems, by shared values, beliefs and interests to the "mother"
country, as was the case with the British Dominions.[7] It is this
federalizing process which has been shaping Puerto Rico's evolu-
tion to statehood.

But there is still an element of uncertainty, when the matter is stated in this way. For if the relationship between states
is described like this, it would also apply to an alliance at one
end, and to a decentralized unitary body at the other. Federalism
is distinguished from these by the fact that in a federal union a
sphere of autonomy for the inclusive community with distinctive spheres of autonomy for the component communities co-
exist.

Autonomy is here taken in its original and basic meaning as the power and the right to govern oneself, to be self-
governed (*auto-nomos!*) in those matters which constitute the
basis of the community. Human beings can and do belong to
several communities of this kind, each autonomous in its own
sphere. Modern as well as Roman absolutism have insisted that
such autonomy is "derived" from the "sovereign," the one
central power, but we believe that the community of family,
church, and neighborhood, to mention only the most basic, are
self-contained. Be that as it may, federalism is an attempt to
institutionalize such local autonomy as an independent and separate power, under a constitution that is the joint creation of

both the inclusive community and the component parts. The autonomy of the component parts is not considered as impaired by participation in the wider community, if the sphere of authority of the wider community is instituted, maintained, and altered only with the effective participation of the component community—as likewise the autonomy of the inclusive community is considered unimpaired, if its sphere cannot be altered without its effective participation. This is the basic core of the idea of a "compact" as the foundation of a federal relationship. It is evident that the intertwining of communities in this fashion will only occur, when a comparable pattern of composite needs and interests, beliefs and values prevails. Hence it is evident, or ought to be, that where the needs and interests, the beliefs and values which divide a component community from the inclusive community of which it forms a part, are distinctive, as is the case of Puerto Rico, a different kind of federal relationship will be needed than that suitable to the rest. There may be, in this case, as in that of the emerging union of Europe, a greater need for restraining the inclusive community and its powers in all but a few select spheres of joint interest, need, and belief.[8] Federalism needs to be seen as a process suited to communities in which the territorially diversified pattern of objectives, interests, needs, and values (traditions) which requires freedom of independence can be effectively implemented and served by joint community efforts in the pursuit of common objectives, interests, needs, and values (the cultivation of common traditions) through freedom of participation. Puerto Rico, by developing the novel status of an associated state, has achieved a substantial amount of both freedoms in all its reaches.

But both these freedoms are in turn composite in nature, because the choices which human beings can make, are of two kinds. They can be *selective* and they can be *creative*. Most of the time, when we speak of freedom, these two possibilities are not clearly distinguished. Yet there is, as far as I can see, a very great difference between choosing between alternatives that are known to exist, and discovering a new alternative by a process of creative invention. Now the freedom of creation, though occurring in both the sphere of personal and communal, of private and public life, is distinct from selection, in that it cannot possibly be predicted.[9] For in order to predict it, one would have to be the inventor which is, strictly speaking, impossible. This is important in connection with the hoary arguments about "freedom of the will." We cannot and do not wish to enter upon this problem here. We are satisfied that beyond all the arguments, including those which insist that it is a "false" problem, there is human action which cannot be predicted, and could not be predicted, even if we knew much more than we do, in short that there is genuine innovation through invention and creation.

The interesting aspect of this dimension of freedom is that its value is transpersonal. Regardless of how one might argue concerning the freedom of making selective choices—the authoritarian restricting it to the few, the antiauthoritarian extending it to the many—freedom of creation is and must be approved. The most autocratic regime will try to find a way of unfettering men for this freedom, at least in those spheres, in which the products of such creation are valued by the rulers, be they artistic, scientific, or technical, or even religious and inspirational. Thus we see the tyrants of Renaissance Italy granting great liberty of creation to artists and writers, and the Soviet Union doing the same for physicists and chemists.

Here, too, what is true of individuals, applies to communities as well. Federalism more particularly seeks to liberate the plural creative impulses and capacities of a culturally variegated people by organizing the government in such a way that maximum autonomy is possible for each component community. The cultural autonomy to which the Puerto Rican people aspire, within their Spanish heritage, is and must be greater than that of communities which form part of the Anglo-American tradition. But far from being an impoverishment of the United States, such freedom of distinctive creativity is an enrichment for all Americans and to be as much welcomed as freedom of creation generally. But not only the more specifically cultural creations in the religious and artistic sense are part of this range of creative freedom; it encompasses the entire political and economic sphere. The production of goods, though more humble in many ways, is the manifestation of the creative impulse on the part of the majority of people and must be maximized within the bounds of organized freedom (see Chapter II).

At this point, it would seem well to say a word more about culture. For culture is a fighting word in the island. Pride in their local culture is a decisive aspect of the Puerto Ricans' concept of association; it is the very core of the commonwealth. The people of Puerto Rico want passionately to preserve their individual personality and being. But they are not at all of one mind concerning this matter. Nor is it always clear what we mean when we talk about culture. To many intellectuals, culture means the sum of literary, artistic, and scientific creations of a people; it means Cervantes, and Velasquez and Goya and Donoso and Unamuno—to illustrate by a few great Spanish names. But these are cultural high points which rest, like the summits of a mountain range, upon the broad foundation of a people's folkways, its way of living, of eating and dressing and making love and having fun. For a people having long lived in penury under colonial tutelage, these folkways are apt to be more significant than what is often called culture with a big C. It too, through the generations, evolves. Just as the English colonies of the mainland developed folkways of their own, long before independence was won from the mother country,[10] Puerto Rico, too, has evolved a local culture which though having deep roots in the Spanish past has become a distinctive thing and continues to evolve over the years. In discussing the problem further, we must bear in mind that we are dealing with culture in all its reaches, including the most lowly.[11]

The Puerto Rican intelligentsia could perhaps be divided into three basic strands: those who see no prospect of maintaining a local culture, and who would promote the complete assimilation and absorption of what remains of it into the North American "melting pot." There are, on the other hand, those who would insist that Puerto Rican culture must disentangle itself from its North American involvements, must throw overboard what has been assimilated, including the English language, and return to its Spanish origins, in close federal association with other Latin-American countries, especially in Central America. And finally there are those who would refuse to do either, and insist that it is Puerto Rico's distinct destiny to go forward on the path of being a bridge between North American and Latin-American culture, blending the two to some extent, but basically evolving its Spanish foundations under the stimulus of North American influences, and in close and continuous cooperation with other Spanish-American countries (who after all are also exposed, though to a lesser extent, to North American influences). In this latter view which is the prevailing one at the present time, and corresponds to the political outlook of the ruling Popular Democratic Party, Puerto Rico provides a meeting ground of two cultures, but should not be confused with either of them.[12] Their feeling corresponds to that of many Swiss who see themselves as a bridge between French and German culture, yet distinctive in both their French-speaking and German-speaking components, and enriched by both cultures without being submerged by either. Anyone familiar with Swiss cultural life will attest to the vitality of this intercultural autonomy, this meeting ground.

For carrying forward that kind of creative cultural autonomy, more independence is required than can be expected within the close-knit context of a federal state dominated by one of the cultures concerned. Swiss individuality would undoubtedly be lost in a relatively short time, if Switzerland were to become part of either the French or the German body politic. And if it happened, it would be a cultural impoverishment of both France and Germany—not to speak of Switzerland herself. If we dig deeper, we discover that the reason for this distinctive cultural individuality must be found in richly variegated folkways that distinguish the everyday life of Swiss folk from that of neighboring Frenchmen and Germans, in spite of the bonds of language which exist.[13]

In this connection, the rapid growth of the University of Puerto Rico may be cited as one clear indication of the vitality of this growing local culture. Nowhere else has so much been accomplished in so little time with such limited resources. The brilliant leadership of the chancellor, a man of great breadth of cultural understanding, and a trained social scientist as well, has made of the university a genuine meeting place of the Spanish- and the English-speaking world. The vigorous criticism which has lately sprung up should, in this case, be seen as a sign of vitality and potentiality of growth. As elsewhere in Puerto Rico, there is little disposition in the university to rest upon one's laurels. It will, of course, take many years to mature the institution. Great universities do require generations for all round ripening. There are weak spots even in the best of them. But it is literally true that without the university, the Commonwealth could not have been built; innumerable are the bonds that bind the university to the various phases of public life, not only through teaching, but also through the fostering of significant research projects. The notes to these pages testify to all this important activity.

It would be tempting to try to sketch all the different cultural spheres in which new life has sprung up since freedom has come to the island. But space does not permit it. There is, however, one activity which is so significant that a word about it is called for, Community Education. Later I shall speak of the weakness of local government and the need for decisive improvement (see pp. 42 ff). This weakness is to some extent compensated for by the activities carried forward under the Division of Community Education. It is an adult education program of unique value. A group of field organizers under able leadership stimulate self-help activities in rural communities. They do not tell the communities what to do, but show them, with the aid of documentary films, radio, books, pamphlets, posters, and lectures and through the stimulation of discussion, what might be done, if the community worked together effectively. It may be a school, or it may be a bridge—the folks are encouraged to seek a solution to the best of their ability. Thus grass roots democracy is slowly being built into the folkways of Puerto Rico —a new cultural ingredient, but one which has ancient roots in the Spanish tradition of the *fuero* of old. If you ask what are the traits of these community organizers, the answer is: "They must be respected at home, catch on to the general idea, dedicate themselves to it, . . ." [14] They act as catalytic agents, showing the humble people in the villages throughout the island what it means to be free.

> In a barrio of Hatillo . . . we have watched the people move from a pressure group, demanding that the mayor . . . solve their problems, to a position where they applauded when a neighbor stated that this was a matter that 'we ourselves must solve.' . . . We were present at a meeting when the members of a community refused graciously but firmly the gift of a large sum of money from a well-to-do person outside their barrio because, they said, they wished to have the opportunity to raise the money

in nickels and dimes from their own pockets. . . . We have watched an influential neighbor try to block a road-building project when he found that the community did not intend to have it pass his store. And then we watched the community win him over to its way of thinking.[15]

These are small matters, but they are the essence of a culture that is "growing into the shoes" of democratic freedom. For such instances indicate the spread of genuine responsibility.

This program illustrates well an aspect of freedom which is often overlooked. Indeed, some of the most bitter controversies in free societies are the result of a lack of understanding of the interdependence of the two kinds of freedom. For it is a peculiarity of freedom that man's desire to maximize it cannot be carried forward both in the direction of independence and of participation. They cannot be jointly maximized, and their creative potential extended at the same time. When the freedom that consists in participating in communal decisions is increased, then independence is thereby reduced.[15a] This is clearly seen in the dilemma of our modern tendency toward collectivization; as spheres of activity are transferred from the private and personal to the public and communal sphere, freedom as independence is reduced. If the total amount of freedom is, under such conditions, to be maintained, it follows that freedom of participation in the public sphere must be expanded. Modern democratic societies provide for such expansion fairly automatically through the provision that all such extensions of the public or collective sphere must be sanctioned by legislative process in which all participate at least indirectly. But very serious problems have arisen, where the legislature has granted extensive discretion to administrators. A bitter controversy is raging over these issues.[16]

Making the specific application to the problem of Puerto Rico, it needs to be said that the very scope of federal legislation makes the question of how to organize Puerto Rican participation in the federal legislative process such a pressing one. The freedom of the people of Puerto Rico is vitally involved in this question. And that means the freedom of every American citizen who moves from the mainland to Puerto Rico. The problem can, of course, be met in two ways. One can either extend the scope of Puerto Rico's share in all federal legislation, which can be done in a variety of ways, short of granting Puerto Rico statehood. Or it can be accomplished by extending Puerto Rico's own sphere of autonomy, thereby removing large areas of selective choices from the federal authorities, as far as Puerto Rico is concerned. Existing proposals tend toward one or another of those solutions.[17]

Regardless of how this dilemma is resolved, it is clear that the autonomy which has been increasingly realized since 1941 has freed vast creative energies that had lain dormant for many a year. This residual aspect of freedom, whether of freedom as independence or of that as participation, is dramatically symbolized in the figure of Puerto Rico's governor, Luis Muñoz Marín. Not only a politician and statesman, but a poet and a philosopher of parts, popular throughout the island as the bard (*el vate*) and convivial companion, Muñoz Marín is a political innovator and inventor of first rank.

In view of the central role which Muñoz Marín has played in the Puerto Rican scene in recent years, it seems justified to offer a brief sketch of his leadership here. This should not be taken to mean that he alone is responsible for what has happened. He would be the first to disown any such claim. Like former Governor, Rexford G. Tugwell on a dramatic occasion, he would probably say that he is not the cause, but the agent of historic forces. But the agent is important. In the case of Muñoz Marín, I do not hesitate to say he is vitally important. His background is intensely political. His father, Muñoz Rivera, was the most prominent figure of his day. Yet, Muñoz Marín has the air of a man of

the people. He has an easy and approachable manner. "Dignified
but never stiff or formal, he has the bearing of command," one of
the ablest students of the island's politics has written. "His voice
is deep and resonant, and he has the kind of face, scarcely to be
described as handsome, which inspires confidence because of its
expression of strength, humor and fellow feeling." [18] His personality is complex. He is friendly, and yet aloof, highly intelli-
gent and yet resistant to notions which do not fit in with his
experience and thought, sincere in basic outlook and yet calcu-
lating and shrewdly expedient in his everyday dealings. He loves
wine and song, and is admired far beyond Puerto Rico in the
Spanish-speaking world as a poet of genuine merit. The vigor
of his imagination, the true gift of the poet, is held in check
by a cautious, even suspicious streak of sharp-eyed circumspec-
tion. While profoundly confident of man's capacity to contribute to his own well-being, he is no builder of utopias, no happy
warrior who would expose himself to unnecessary risks. His
humor is strong and ever-ready, but it is a somewhat sardonic
one, familiar from Cervantes as a Spanish heritage.

With such a personality it is not surprising that Muñoz
Marín should have become the remarkable inspirational leader
that he is today. The common humble folk of the island worship him and many call themselves *Muñocistas,* followers of
Muñoz. His leadership is genuinely democratic in the sense of
being a two-way relationship; he is no disguised élitist who considers himself as separate and apart from the masses whom he
represents. His speeches are simple and direct, enlivened by a
ready wit and reinforced by manly strength. He is as quintes-
sentially Puerto Rican and Spanish, as Abraham Lincoln was
American: to the manner born.

"Within the political élite Muñoz is acknowledged even by
his opponents to stand head and shoulders above everybody else.
The brilliance of his conversation, the fertility of ideas, the

shrewdness of his judgment of men and affairs, and the range
of his knowledge, interests, and connections set him off. . . ."
This outlook is always to be found, where a potent leader
achieves predominance. Among the younger group there seem
to me to be a number of men who given time and opportunity
may rival Muñoz Marín's leadership. But this is merely said
in order to avoid the kind of hero worship that tends to distort
the free development of political life.

Characteristically, Muñoz Marín has remarked that "to
govern is to invent." He himself has certainly lived up to this
maxim. It is a thoroughly American idea—one to which the men
of Philadelphia would have heartily assented. Benjamin Franklin
is the human symbol of this inventiveness; he would have been
proud of his Puerto Rican fellow citizens. But among all the
many innovations, one stands out even though it is as yet incom-
plete and in urgent need of further work. It is the idea of free
association, transcending that of federal union.

The new status of Puerto Rico as a free and associated state
or commonwealth is a new dimension of federal government.
Nothing like it was envisaged by the fathers of the American
Constitution. They still thought in terms of a simple territorial
entity, composed of "states and territories." We pointed out
above how this great invention of federalism which was accomplished at Philadelphia could be more broadly interpreted as a
process of federalizing composite communities. Association, as
a new dimension of federalism, is not confined to Puerto Rico,
however; indeed, it may be seen as a world-wide trend. More
especially in Europe, highly flexible arrangements for "associat-
ing" Britain and other European powers with the Coal and
Steel Community, as well as with the Common Market Community, are in the making. Their case is similar to that of
Puerto Rico, in that they are not ready for close federal union
even in limited fields. West Berlin's curious form of participa-

tion in the German Federal Republic is another example. But it is clear that the Puerto Rican situation exhibits unique features.[19] These will be more fully explored in the next chapter. Suffice it to say here that it places the old federal principle of "unity with diversity" on a new basis. There is more independence and less participation, but both kinds of freedom are being provided in increasing measure, thus giving ample scope to creativity. Puerto Rico's emergent status as a free and associated state thus conceivably provides a new model for future developments in the sphere of the liberation of colonial peoples who do not wish or may not be able to organize themselves as independent political communities, yet may not wish to be absorbed into a fully integrated federal union.[20] Voices have already been heard which would thus associate substantial portions of Africa in the future with the European federal union that is in the making. The proposed European political community aroused suspicion and criticism, because it would merely envisage the possibility that such dependent territories might in the future apply for membership in the federation.[21]

Having now clarified, we hope, the novelty and the significance of the Puerto Rican achievement, when looked at from the vantage point of freedom, in its several aspects, it remains to inquire, how this new kind of federal compact, this new balance of the two kinds of freedom, is related to justice. For if the previous colonial status was manifestly unjust, the new condition of Puerto Rico as a free and associated commonwealth, while less unjust, may yet fall short of providing for full justice. We do, indeed, believe this to be the case, and shall show in the last chapter how it ought to be changed. But let us see what this argument about justice means.[22]

Obviously, it is not a question of what is legal. As in any period of rapid social change, the existing law cannot serve as a basis for judgment as to what is just. I should like to leave aside such lofty metaphysical notions as are embodied in the doctrines of Plato and the Roman Catholic church, since they presuppose an élite who are in possession of the truth. How then can justice be determined? Ever since Aristotle, it has been recognized that central to the problem of justice is that of equality. To be just, is to give to equals equal rewards, penalties, and the like. Therefore, he who decides in a community who shall be equal to whom, is determining the basis of justice. Thus what distinguishes the radical democrats from the defenders of wealth and privilege is the insistence that all men are basically equal, that the small differences between them are the result of environment, and do not deserve the attention of the government. Modern politics has tried to sidestep this basic decision by declaring that men are "equal before the law." But that merely shifts the ground. For if the answer now becomes: the people, through their representatives, determine the law, then it follows that they determine who is equal to whom and what therefore is just.

By such a reference to this kind of decision the problem of justice is evidently not solved. But it is clear that it cannot be solved without the people's participation. In its application to the Puerto Rican scene, it means that even though justice may not result, if the Puerto Rican people make their own laws, or at least participate in the making of them, it *cannot* even be discovered without such participation.

At this point it becomes manifest how closely the problem of justice is tied to that of freedom, participating freedom. Freedom of independence, on the other hand, may be the source of great injustice, when it removes from the reach of law what may call for a redistribution of advantages. It shows at the same time, how intimately both are bound up with the cultural background and value judgments of a people. What determines equality, and hence justice, cannot be considered without determining what constitutes inequality. Among a people who value artistic creation above all else, the artist will be considered more deserving of differential rewards than among one who prefer economic and technological creativity, or an imposing array of distinguished ancestors.

But there is a problem hidden here which is often overlooked. It results from the view taken of the people. If the people are seen merely as a conglomeration of interest groups, each pursuing its own aim, then the law, and hence the decision about equality and justice, is purely a resultant of the parallelogram of forces at work in such a society. Only if it can be asserted that in any free community there exist a sufficient number of responsible and conscientious persons who seek to find solutions transcending the particular interests, the crystallization of just decisions is conceivable. The American doctrine of the common man, as the community-conscious citizen who decisively shapes politics in the free community, is built upon this view.[23]

This faith has once again been amply justified by recent events in Puerto Rico. No sooner was a measure of genuine freedom acquired than lawmaking in the general interest developed at a rapid pace. The pressure of special interests has not been absent, of course. Corruption has appeared here and there. Yet, the story of Puerto Rico's public life shows the common man on the march.

The maximizing of freedom through genuine autonomy for the people of Puerto Rico and freedom of independence for its citizens as individuals, and the consequent liberation of creative impulses manifesting themselves in political and governmental innovation no more than in economic production, and social and cultural growth, have not only made Puerto Rico a healthy community. They have prevented the spread of communism in the island. Although material conditions in Puerto

Rico at the beginning of the postwar period would seem to have offered an ideal opportunity for Communist infiltration, such as has occurred in some Caribbean islands, notably the French possessions, the Communist following in Puerto Rico is as minimal as it is in the rest of the United States. Their attempt to bolster their fortunes by association with terrorist nationalist elements has borne no fruit; the *Independentistas* certainly were most anxious to dissociate themselves from so unwelcome an ally. In this respect, also, the Puerto Rican experience has important lessons for other troubled areas.

In light of what has been said in this introductory review, it ought to be clear why Puerto Rico's political, economic, and cultural position may justly be described as embodying a unique contribution to the solution of the problem of how to combine freedom and justice. How this feat was accomplished in government and politics is the story to which we shall turn in our next chapter.

NOTES

1. A study of this Declaration is found in H. Lauterpacht, *International Law and Human Rights* (1950), pp. 428 ff. For the text, see *UN Yearbook* (1948–1949). It should be noted that the attempt to embody its principles in the Puerto Rican constitution was rejected by the U.S. Congress; what was acceptable as a pious declaration, was not so as an enforceable part of American government— a revealing bit of political disillusionment.

2. This discussion of the status of Puerto Rico before the UN Trusteeship Council is found in the record as cited below, Chapter III, note 5. See also Emil J. Sady, *The United Nations and Dependent Peoples*, The Brookings Institution (1956).

3. *Research on Freedom—Report of Dialectical Discoveries and Constructions* by The Institute for Philosophical Research, directed by Mortimer Adler, in two volumes (1954), esp. pp. 62 ff. The first of these has now appeared as a book: *Idea of Freedom* (1958).

4. *Op. cit.*, p. 520. The authors state that "freedom is understood as

involving *independence of something other than the self.*" I wonder whether it would not be more correct to speak of this as "independence *from anything*"; for on their own evidence the authors exclude dependence on anything other than the self. See for this my comments in "Political Philosophy and the Science of Politics" in *Approaches to the Study of Politics* (1958).

The authors built their discussion of the general agreement upon the "discovery" of three "nuclear agreements," that is to say, three kinds of freedom, namely: (a) circumstantial; (b) natural; and (c) acquired freedom. The concept of circumstantial freedom stresses that circumstances inhibiting or promoting human action determine the degree of independence and hence of freedom; that of natural freedom the inborn ability of men as men to originate what they do; that of acquired freedom the capacity for self-perfection.

5. Cf. Jakob Burckhardt, *Griechische Kulturgeschichte*, (ed., Staehelin), p. 80 and elsewhere. A similar view was taken by Fustel de Coulanges, *The Ancient City* (English, 7th ed., 1889), p. 298: "It is a singular error therefore, to believe that in the ancient cities men enjoyed liberty. They had not even the idea of it. They did not believe that there could exist any rights as against the city and its gods. . . . To have political rights, to vote, to name magistrates, to have the privilege of being archon,—this was called liberty; but man was not the less enslaved to the state." Even though somewhat exaggerated, Fustel de Coulanges' conclusions on this score are well worth remembering.

6. Regarding this "basic experience" see the book cited below, note 22.

7. Cf. my paper in *Federalism, Mature and Emergent* (ed., Arthur McMahon, 1955), entitled "Federal Constitutional Theory and Emergent Proposals"; cf. also the interesting review of the earlier proposals by Arturo Morales Carrión "The Commonwealth of Puerto Rico—Its Historical Roots and Present Significance," a paper presented at the Eighth Annual Conference on the Caribbean, University of Florida, December 6, 1957.

8. Further elaboration of these points will be found in my paper just cited. This view has been fitted into the recent revision of the federalism chapter of my *Constitutional Government and Democracy* published in France under the title *La Democratie Constitutionelle* (1958).

9. See Maurice Cranston, *Freedom—A New Analysis* (1953) and my comments in a volume entitled *Approaches to the Study of Politics* (1958), "Political Philosophy and the Science of Politics."

10. Cf. Perry Miller, *The New England Mind* (1939); John C. Miller, *Origins of the American Revolution* (1943), esp. ch. VIII; Carl Becker, *The Declaration of Independence* (1951), and Kaethe Spiegel, *Kulturgeschichtliche Grundlagen der Amerikanischen Revolution* (1931).

11. Julian H. Steward and Associates, *The People of Puerto Rico* (1956). Cf. for the basic approach, A. L. Kroeber, ed., *Anthropology Today* (1956), esp. p. XIV.

12. A fine, balanced statement is offered by Francisco Ayala, "Puerto Rico—Un Destino Ejemplar" from *Cuadernos Americanos* (1951). See also E. Fernández Méndes, "Bases para una política de la cultura y de la educación en la Democracia" (MS.), 1957.

13. Among the books dealing with this problem, I would especially recommend Robert C. Brooks, *Civic Training in Switzerland* (1930).

14. As quoted in E. P. Hanson, *Transformation* (1955), p. 348. The whole chapter is very informative, though perhaps overstressing the motion pictures, and a bit dithyrambic.

15. Hanson, *op. cit.*, p. 350.

15a. The following reflection will show the reason why. If the entire range of selective choices be A, and if these choices be either personal and private ($p1$) or communal and public ($p2$), then A evidently equals $p1$ plus $p2$. Hence if A is a determinate number, no matter of what magnitude, an increase in the number of $p1$ must mean a decrease in the number of $p2$.

16. See William A. Robson, *Justice and Administrative Law* (1st. ed., 1928), and G. W. Keeton, *The Passing of Parliament* (1952), among others.

17. Cf. the speech by Muñoz Marín, at Kansas University, April 23, 1955. Since then, the discussion has continued. See Chapter III.

18. Cf. Henry Wells, "Ideology and Leadership in Puerto Rican Politics" in *American Political Science Review* XLIX (1955), pp. 22 ff. at 32. Cf. also E. P. Hanson, *Transformation* (1955), ch. VI. The next quotation is also found in Wells.

19. The revisions in the theory of federalism which are called for by these and related developments are explored by the author in "Fed-

eral Constitutional Theory and Emergent Proposals" in *Federalism, Mature and Emergent* (1955), edited by Arthur McMahon (1955), pp. 510 ff.

20. Besides quite a few private and semipublic (organizational) proposals, there is the official draft treaty of the so-called Ad Hoc Assembly, prepared in 1953, for the establishment of a European Political Community, which, even though it was prevented from further consideration by the collapse of the European Defense Community plans, remains a seminal document of lasting significance. It can be found as Appendix II in *Studies in Federalism*, directed and edited by Robert R. Bowie and Carl J. Friedrich (1954).

21. These perspectives were preliminarily explored by the author in "The World Significance of the New Constitution" in *The Annals*, vol. 285, entitled *Puerto Rico—A Study in Democratic Development* (1953), edited by Millard Hansen and Henry Wells. The paper is found at pp. 42 ff.

22. See for this my *Legal Philosophy in Historical Perspective* (1958), ch. XX. This is the English version of a book published in 1955 in German.

23. See for this my *The New Belief in the Common Man* (1942), enlarged edition entitled *The New Image of the Common Man* (1951); of this edition a Spanish version, *La Nueva Imagen del Hombre Común*, has just been published (1958).

2

Absolute Autonomy
for Puerto Rico

Neither of a man nor of a people—which is in a certain sense also a man—can a change be demanded which breaks the unity and continuity of the person.

Miguel de Unamuno
THE TRAGIC SENSE OF LIFE, Ch. 1

THE CONCEPT of genuine autonomy, rooted in the dignity, the very personality of individuals and groups, radically differs from the concept which was once a political slogan in the islands. In the struggle for a measure of self-government under the Spanish Crown, autonomy, as the Autonomist Party conceived of it, referred to a power and authority derived from Spain, and dependent upon its central power. Such "autonomy" is not truly self-rule, because it is not truly self-constituted. The autonomy which we have in mind is genuine, it is a manifestation of a community's self. It is what the men who demanded "sovereignty" for the states at Philadelphia had in mind, and what the states still possess within the federal union. This "sovereignty" is, of course, something very different from what is usually understood by this term: the complete independence, so-called, of national states in the international realm. Indeed, if it were not for this now prevailing usage, there is no reason why we should not continue to talk of "sovereignty" in describ-

25

ing the partially fulfilled aspiration of Puerto Rico. But since
"sovereignty" now stands as the symbol of that anachronistic
state of international anarchy, and since even in Europe, where
the idea was first developed, great nations strive to overcome it
and to associate in a more comprehensive union, it would do
Puerto Rico less than justice to describe its emergent order as
"sovereign." Still, if anyone would be happy to use this term,
rather than autonomy, absolute autonomy, I would understand.
But as was shown in the previous chapter, the emerging world
order is such that the concept of the autonomy of federally
united communities seems more appropriate.

Freedom is self-realization, or rather self-fulfillment. This
is as true for a community, as it is for the individual. It needs
freedom to achieve its creative potential. Complete freedom is no
more possible for a community than for an individual. All self-
expression is limited by counterclaims for self-expression by
others. In the relations between so-called sovereign states, it is
often difficult to strike the just balance. When such efforts fail,
war results. If war is considered too great a price to pay for
such maintenance of the community's self, in relation to certain
other communities, a union of states seeks to provide a framework for freedom within which rival claims can be suitably
adjusted and common purposes achieved through joint action.
A measure of unity is combined with a maximum of diversity
in such a scheme; it is the essence of federalism. The great range
of possible balances has given federalism its scope and variety.
One of the most enduring programs for federalizing a variegated
community structure was devised at Philadelphia in 1787. It is a
proud heritage.[1]

The makers of the Constitution certainly never dreamed
of anything like the political development that is Puerto Rico
today. No more than they thought of the Interstate Commerce
Commission when they wrote the Interstate Commerce Clause,

or dozens of other comparably important developments. When they were laboring at Philadelphia, Puerto Rico was a colony of the Spanish Crown, held in autocratic subjection by that ancient feudal monarchy. Then in the course of the nineteenth century, as liberalism spread throughout Europe, and constitutionalized Spain with the rest, the spirit of independence seized the peoples throughout Spanish America. One by one, led by passionate lovers of freedom such as Simon Bolivár, they achieved independence and sovereignty. But Puerto Rico, though tempted to follow the same path, had sought freedom within the Spanish realm. These efforts had just begun to bear fruit, with a substantial measure of dependent, local autonomy attained, when the Spanish-American War brought the island under American control. Hailed as liberators and bringers of a new day of freedom, the Americans soon proved that they had no conception of such freedom.

Unfamiliar with colonial problems, intoxicated by a temporary flurry of imperialist sentiment about their "manifest destiny," they proceeded to treat the proud Spanish population much as they had been in the habit of treating the American Indian—as a ward entitled to a measure of material welfare, but certainly not ready for the kind of freedom which they were ready to grant any Spanish immigrant who came to America. It is a strange inconsistency, this readiness to cherish a vigorous "statue-of-liberty-idealism" for any and all within the continental United States, combined with an equal readiness to withhold it from those who had come under American jurisdiction by conquest and the power of the sword. Lest we forget the extent of our commitment, let us recall that when General Miles landed in Puerto Rico on July 25, 1898, he stated that his forces came "bearing the banner of freedom . . ." and bringing "the fostering arm of a nation of free people, whose greatest power is in justice and humanity to all those living in its fold." Americans had not "come to make war . . . but to bring protection, to promote . . . prosperity, and to bestow . . . the immunities and blessings of the liberal institutions of our government." [2] Had Americans at the turn of the century been as sensitively alert to universal human claims to freedom, as they are today, when criticizing their friends the French in Algeria, or the British in Cyprus, history might have taken a very different course, and Puerto Rico might be today either a flourishing state of the Union, or an independent state, such as Haiti. Or they might even have carried forward the work, so auspiciously begun by Spanish and Puerto Rican liberals, and developed what we see today, namely a free and associated state. But the time was not ripe for such a radical innovation, and much sweat and tears, as well as a little blood, had to be shed, before this became possible.[3]

I shall pass over here in silence the nearly fifty years of American colonial rule, characterized by a slow improvement in some material conditions, a rapid decline in others, and culminating in the desperate state of affairs so vividly and compassionately portrayed by R. Tugwell.[4] By 1938, the situation had come to a real impasse. The standard of living of the masses was abysmally low, way below that of even the poorest state of the Union—a matter to which we shall return in the next chapter. Local political leadership had been locked in a desperate, fruitless struggle over the question of status. Whether Puerto Rico should seek independence or statehood, that seemed *the* question, as the partisans, especially of independence, became ever more violent. Yet there was little sense in either position. For the Congress and the people of the United States showed small disposition to grant statehood even to the incorporated territories of Alaska and Hawaii. Prevailing sentiment was expressed with brutal frankness by a perhaps apocryphal Senator at the time, when the new solution was being discussed. Said he:

"Give them anything, as long as they do not want to be a state." Congress might be ready to grant independence, as they had just done for the Philippines. But how was this overcrowded island, with its economy tightly linked to that of the United States and the mainland taking some of its surplus population, ever going to survive, if its bonds with the U.S. were severed? Really, *Independentistas* and *Estadistas* were presenting with a vengeance a Hobson's choice to the starving people of Puerto Rico. As Muñoz Marín was to put it drily: "If we seek statehood, we die waiting for Congress, and if we adopt independence, we die from starvation—in any case, we die." [5] Muñoz Marín therefore decided to found a new party which he called the Popular Democratic Party which was to be dedicated to fostering the welfare of the Puerto Rican people, rather than concern itself with the problem of status. But they soon discovered that it was not possible to accomplish major innovations in the economic field without similar changes in the political and governmental field. Since the old dichotomy of statehood versus independence was as sterile as ever, they turned to the task of inventing new solutions, commencing with the elective governor and culminating in the constitution of a free and associated commonwealth, based upon a contract between the people of Puerto Rico and the rest of the American people, as represented in the Congress.

The proposal to elect their own governor was formally made to the Congress by President Roosevelt in March 1943.[6] It had been under discussion for some time, and Tugwell had hinted at it in a statement some nine months earlier. The proposal was enacted into law in 1947 after extended debates,[7] the ground having being prepared by appointment as governor, in 1946 of Sr. Piñero, a widely respected native Puerto Rican. Congress, in fact, expected him to be elected. Under the Jones Act, Puerto Ricans had become citizens of the United States, had enjoyed the protection of a bill of rights and had continued to elect their own legislature, consisting of two houses, and authorized to deal with "local legislation," but subject to the veto of the presidentially appointed governor. The act also had provided for a resident commissioner to the United States, elected by the people of the island.[8] It is evident, both from this structure and from the story of the actual working of the Organic Act, that it granted the people of the island an insufficient amount even of dependent autonomy, not only because laws adopted by the legislature and presumably expressing the popular will, were recurrently vetoed by the governors,[9] but also because the possibility of veto hampered and often frustrated the formation of such a will. Indeed, the arrangement served as a cloak, behind which undemocratic forces of special interest could entrench themselves. As Tugwell put it, in a radio address in 1942, "the New Deal never properly came to Puerto Rico . . . most of the Island's people remained sunk in helpless poverty. The efforts that were made to lift her out of this morass . . . were more or less successfully defeated . . . by the small group of reactionaries who dominated the economic and political life. . . ."[10] This may have been something of an exaggeration; but there can be no doubt that the economy of the island was stagnant at the end of the thirties (see below).

Why was making the governorship elective the decisive step? I believe it was because it enabled the people to become united in support of dynamic political leadership, as personified by Luis Muñoz Marín. But merely the election of the governor was not enough. For even though the people could now voice clearly their needs and aspirations, the island's government remained hamstrung by its dependence upon the goodwill of the government of the United States and more particularly of the Congress. Genuine "absolute" autonomy could not be said to exist, as long as the government of the island was "by the grace" of the Congress. Autonomy means that the *nomos*, the basic legal and governmental framework of a community is its own creation and hence *self-made*. Nothing short of a constitution, freely adopted by the people themselves, could provide such autonomy. There certainly existed in the island the makings of a genuine constituent group. But how could that group be given the *power* to fulfill its task? [11] The road of statehood was barred, as we have seen. There seemed to exist no provision, under the United States Constitution, for allowing a group of American citizens, not citizens of a state, to establish their own constitution. The only way to accomplish it would seem an amendment, implementing the Constitution,[12] but this would take years, as the history of constitutional amendments in America clearly shows. So the unusual device was adopted of asking the Congress to agree to grant the people of Puerto Rico the power to adopt their own constitution. By adopting Public Law 600 of 1950, the Congress entered into a solemn agreement, "in the nature of a compact," with the people of Puerto Rico, whereunder they in exchange for continued allegiance to the United States received the authority to elect a constituent assembly, and to adopt its proposals for a constitution, if approved by the President and Congress.[13] No need here to describe in detail the devoted work by experts and political leadership alike that went into this historic task. Suffice it to say that a constitution was brought into being in the short span of a little more than a year (1951–1952), but unfortunately not without the Congress striking from the proposal parts of the bill of rights, as previously mentioned.

The steps of this historic transition were simple. First, the Congress adopted Public Law 600, providing for a consultation of the Puerto Rican people as to whether they wanted to go forward toward constitutional self-government within the framework of the U.S. Constitution and elect a constituent assembly. This the people in a referendum on June 4, 1951, affirmatively answered. 76.5 per cent of those voting approved the act, 65 per cent of the voters participating in the referendum. On August 27, 1951, the constituent assembly was elected, ninety-two delegates in all.* The convention thus elected prepared a constitution during the winter of 1951–1952 which was approved by 375,000 voters, not quite 50 per cent of the electorate. It was then submitted to the President and Congress, and after their approval, it was presented to the Puerto Rican legislature for the final ratification which they gave, so that on July 25, 1952, the existence of the Commonwealth could be officially proclaimed. There can be little doubt that a majority of the people approved the constitution. To be sure, no absolute majority of the electorate voted affirmatively, in this referendum, and the opposition has continued to dwell on this fact. But this is true of a great many referenda, both in America and Europe and it must be assumed that those not voting are willing to acquiesce in the decision of the more active citizenry.[14]

The constitution as adopted is placed within the framework of Public Law 600 which is based upon the concept that the people of Puerto Rico are governed by their own consent. In addition to authorizing the drafting and adoption of a constitution, P.L. 600 preserved certain parts of the Organic Act of 1917 and designated them the Puerto Rican Federal Relations Act. The sections of the Organic Act which remain in effect under this new title are urgently in need of clarification and revision. They are those dealing with American citizenship, federal property, applicability of federal laws, free trade with

* It should be noted, however, that the *Independentistas*, representing between 10 and 15 per cent of the electorate, refused to elect delegates to the convention, as they had previously refused to participate in the referendum. But this maneuver, patently designed to obscure their limited support and to produce the impression that all those not voting were of their opinion, should mislead few people.

the mainland, exemption from payment of U.S. internal revenues, the transfer of internal revenues to the Puerto Rican Treasury when paid by other Americans on Puerto Rican products, a similar transfer of customs dues collected in Puerto Rico on foreign imports, the provisions concerning the resident commissioner, the relation of the Puerto Rican judicial system to the federal judiciary, the privileges and immunities of U.S. citizens residing in Puerto Rico, who are not Puerto Rican citizens, the imposition of taxes on exports, the sale of Puerto Rican bonds in the U.S., as well as certain "colonial" restrictions, that should be removed, such as reports to the federal government, debt and tax limits, qualifications for Puerto Rican citizenship, and the like.[15]

It is unfortunate that this framework is so unsatisfactory; in my opinion a review and revisions are overdue. Its main failures are as follows: (1) failure to provide for Puerto Rican participation in the process of federal legislation, when made applicable to Puerto Rico; (2) failure to provide for participation in the fields of foreign affairs, international relations, and defense; (3) failure to envisage a contribution by Puerto Rico to the federal treasury; (4) failure to give Puerto Rico the same freedom as other states regarding a number of local matters, such as citizenship and the debt; and (5) failure to enable the people of Puerto Rico to develop its own bill of rights, within the provisions of the federal Constitution. As for the first, I should add that any applicable federal laws should, if at all possible, be locally administered, delegated administration having proved feasible under such conditions elsewhere. The excuse or if you please justification usually offered for these serious limitations upon Puerto Rican freedom, both of independence and participation, is that Puerto Ricans do not pay federal income and other taxes, although receiving federal benefits under a variety of programs. But is not Puerto Rican participation in the defense of the United States, is not the blood of her sons, far more important than any amount of dollars, and the true basis of full citizenship?

Before examining the constitution and the government operating under it, as well as the politics which gives this constitution and government its life and vitality, a word needs to be said about the vexing question as to whether the Congress could abolish the status granted to Puerto Rico as a free and associated state? Related to this question is the further one, whether the Supreme Court could declare this settlement "unconstitutional." Let us consider the second question first. If one considers the entire range of legislation that the Supreme Court has from time to time held unconstitutional, it becomes apparent that most of such legislation was claimed to be a violation of "individual" rights, some of it a violation of "states' rights." Due process, equal protection, and related issues have been in the forefront of this constitutional review. The legislation concerning Puerto Rico has been outside this sphere. The questions which have come before courts, more especially before the U.S. Circuit Court,[16] have been answered in such a way as to uphold Congressional action in this field. There is the further consideration, stressed in recent years, which would give legislative action the benefit of the doubt to the furthest possible extent, except where individual rights are clearly threatened. Finally there is the well-known doctrine of "political" issues; for it is certainly arguable, from the entire record, that the decision of Congress to enter into this agreement with the people of Puerto Rico was a "political decision." While it would be going beyond the evidence to say that the Supreme Court *could not* hold this legislation unconstitutional, it is clear that it is extremely unlikely that it *would* do so. To be sure, the action of the Congress may eventually require a restatement or enlargement of the doctrine laid down in earlier decisions,[17] and it seems doubtful whether in doing so, the court would abandon the proposition that Puerto Rico is a territory of the United States. This is due to the fact that the Constitution only recognizes states (as defined by the Constitution itself) and territories. But it may well develop, beyond the present distinction of incorporated and unincorporated territories, the concept of a self-governing territory as the term applicable to the Commonwealth of Puerto Rico. There are, at present, deep resentments felt in the island against such a proposition, and one might well hope for that reason, that no occasion will arise for arguing such an issue. But whatever the term applied to it, judicial interpretation has so far accepted the new status and is likely to continue to do so.

Could Congress, then, abolish the present status? It has been argued that as a consequence of the ancient doctrine about no parliament being able to bind future parliaments, any future Congress remains free to undo the work of the Eighty-second. But this proposition is defective in several ways. First, the alleged doctrine is not absolute; in reference to particular matters, including property rights and other kinds of contractual relations, such as specifically similar grants made to colonial territories by the British Parliament, the doctrine has not been maintained.[18] Second, successive Congresses have considered themselves bound by agreements entered into in connection with former territories that became states.[19] Third, the grant of the status of an associated state may be placed in analogy to the grant of independence, may therefore be seen as in some ways subject to the rules of international law and treaties. Congress has always considered itself bound by treaty obligations, and the doctrine of *rebus sic stantibus*[20] is not acknowledged by the United States as good international law. To these legal considerations may be added the expedient one that

Congress would not, even if it could do so in law, try to undo such a step, because it would be too manifestly an attempt at unscrambling a finished omelet.

Let us assume, then, that the present status is reasonably secure, and remember that no human creation ever is more than that. What are the significant features of the government of Puerto Rico today? At the outset, I want to emphasize once more that Puerto Rico is governed by the federal government of the United States in all those paramount matters that are part of the national fabric. Puerto Rico is covered and protected by American foreign policy. Puerto Ricans serve in the armed forces of the United States, in peace and in war. The currency of the U.S. is legal currency in the island, and its postal tariff, its stamps are those of the U.S.—not an unimportant matter for an island, when the difference between domestic and foreign airmail letters is nearly 100 per cent. Puerto Ricans can freely go anywhere in the United States, and the produce of their labor can be shipped anywhere in the United States, without customs duties being levied against them, likewise any goods manufactured in the United States can come to Puerto Rico unencumbered. Many federal programs, conferring benefits upon United States citizens, in agriculture, education, and social security, to mention only three major ones, are made applicable to Puerto Rico, and hence benefit the island. This is not an exhaustive list of the fields of modern administration in which the federal authorities govern the island, but they suggest the magnitude of these activities. Truly they affect the life of every Puerto Rican every day of his life. The fact that all these activities are carried forward by officials appointed without the consent of Puerto Rico, that the policies which they express are adopted without the consent of Puerto Rico, indicates the severe limits within which autonomy is at present defined. They suggest the importance of radical alterations in the federal relations we believe to be necessary before Puerto Rico can be considered truly self-governing. But along with these federal governing activities, we find today a growing sphere of true self-government in the island. To this sphere and how it is organized we now turn.

The government of Puerto Rico is in pattern a typical American state government. Suggestions at the time the constitution was adopted to the effect that it might be suitable, both in view of the island's electorate and the Spanish tradition, to adopt a parliamentary form of government of the British type, fell on deaf ears. The people of Puerto Rico were and wanted to be Americans. Besides, the presence of a popularly elected legislature and a presidentially appointed governor had accustomed Puerto Ricans to that kind of separation of powers, just as it had done in America in colonial days [21]; for what it is worth, we might add that even Spanish rule in the nineteenth century had followed this pattern. No less important than the executive-legislative design, that is to say, the presidential type of democracy, is the judicially enforced pattern of a bill-of-rights framework for such a government. The judicial system of Puerto Rico is perhaps the most advanced in the U.S. today, all judicial bodies in the island constituting for administrative purposes one court, presided over by the Chief Justice of the Supreme Court. Judges are appointed by the governor, however, on the basis of a complex advisory procedure in which professional judgment of the bench and bar is marshaled.[22]

The legislature is composed of two houses, a senate and a house, but in view of the present party situation this bicameral system does not seem to make much sense. We should remember, however, that the situation may change. The legislature is vigorously led by the governor who as president of the dominant party controls all the essential levers of power. Most legislation, including the budget, of course, is drafted in the executive establishment which consists of a number of department heads, appointed by the governor with the consent of the senate.[23] On the whole, the work of the legislature is good; certainly it compares well with the work of other American state legislatures. But the Puerto Rican legislature does not conceive of itself as the policy-making body, even to the limited extent to which American state legislatures do.[24]

It would be tedious to review, in textbook fashion, the details of the organization and work of the Puerto Rican legislature. It resembles in many respects other American state legislatures, thus testifying to the fact that the liberal political culture of constitutionalism is a common possession of western Europe and America. There are, however, unique features distinguishing Puerto Rican legislative work which deserve brief comment. They are, largely, the consequence of Puerto Rican inventiveness rather than a consequence of Spanish tradition. First, I would mention the deliberate efforts to protect the minority, for example by filling vacancies through appointment upon nomination by the party,[25] or by always providing for committee membership of the minorities.[26] Second, I would mention the unique provision of treating the entire four years of a legislature's incumbency as one continuous session, with the result that bills can be carried over and their effective handling thus insured.[27] Altogether, Puerto Rico has rather efficient modern procedures, exemplified in their substituting a single reading for the old cumbersome three readings. There can be little doubt that these procedures are at least in part responsible for the steady improvement in legislative work since the Commonwealth constitution went into effect.[28] Another reason is, of course, that the legislature gradually is developing habits of constructive work in lieu of obstruction and criticism. North American legislators will be a bit envious to hear that there is very little pressure group activity, due largely to the discipline of the party and vigorous executive leadership for the legislative program of each year.[29] Another very admirable reform is in the field of apportionment. An effort has been made to remove reapportionment as far from political maneuvers as possible, by taking it out of the hands of the legislators themselves, who as interested parties ought not to be in charge, and putting it into semijudicial hands, with explicit provision that election districts must be contiguous and compact, yet must be reviewed regularly, regardless of party political "vested interests." No rotten boroughs in Puerto Rico, nor gerrymanders either! [30]

Not strictly a part of the legislature, and yet an important part of its operational task of controlling the expenses of public authorities on behalf of the taxpayer is the office of the controller. This office has been developed to a remarkable degree in Puerto Rico, and its occupant is one of the highest paid and most important public servants in the Commonwealth. His position, though he is nominally responsible to the legislature, is very independent. By not merely reporting to the legislature and to the government agencies concerned, but by making public releases to the press, the controller has become what has aptly been called "the keeper of the government's conscience." [31] In a Commonwealth in which power is so highly concentrated, the development of such an office testifies to the Puerto Ricans' political maturity and sound judgment. There are, however, inherent dangers which may at some point, when party passions run high, give serious trouble. The office of the controller "could become a formidable instrument of injustice. . . . If the controller were guided by partisan or unscrupulous motives, his power of publicity could be exercised in such a way as to destroy the reputations and ruin the lives of able and reliable public servants. . . . the power would seem to be justifiable only if it is used with scrupulous care and restraint. . . ." So far, Puerto Rico has been lucky in having it so exercised for the common good, i.e., the prevention of dishonesty in government and the promotion of greater effectiveness.

All in all, we may justly conclude from this brief enumeration of novel features of the legislature and its work in Puerto Rico that at any rate in this sphere autonomy has yielded substantial benefits to all concerned. The extent to which the freedom of effective participation has been put to constructive use and caused beneficial innovation is one more instance where Lord Acton's famous dictum about power has not proved true. Power, and highly concentrated power at that, has not "corrupted" here at all; on the contrary, existing corruption has to some considerable extent been eliminated. For if power at times corrupts, the absence of it, where needed for essential tasks, may also be "corrupting" in the most dangerous sense.

From the legislature, we turn to the governor and the executive establishment, clearly both formally and in fact the keystone of the Puerto Rican self-government.[32] Rooted in the colonial past, as we have noted, the governor, now elected by the people with great majorities, is the real ruler of the island. Or rather, it is through him that the people of Puerto Rico rule themselves. It is in his person and his office that the unique achievement of Puerto Rico's autonomy is most signally symbolized. For the governor is both formally and informally the man in whom the new freedom of the Puerto Rican people is most fully implemented and realized. He is not only the chief executive, and as such "head of the state," but he is the chief policy formulator, both in his capacity as chief administrator and party chief. It is of course his dynamic leadership of his broadly based party which must be considered the primary source of his power. Whether other men, following him, can achieve a similar leadership and thus fulfill his role, remains to be seen. There are many able men in and out of the government of Puerto Rico today, but none of them possesses the broad support of Muñoz

Marín, nor could they, while he is the effective leader of the party.

There may be some serious danger ahead, should the present party fall apart or be replaced by another as the island's outlook and viewpoint change. A serious weakness of the constitution may yet be revealed by those of its provisions whereby the governor, and the resident commissioner, as well as both houses of the legislature are elected every four years. For this arrangement may mean a radical transfer of power, with a consequent lack of any continuity whatsoever. Since all heads of executive establishments from the secretary of state on down are appointed by the governor (with the advice and consent of the senate) except that the secretary of state and the controller in addition require the consent of the house, a radical transformation may mean disaster, if the governor should not possess outstanding qualifications for his many-sided office.[33] But at present, the extraordinary concentration of power in the hands of the governor is working well. I might mention here a singular feature of the government of Puerto Rico which has not yet come into play, and that is the absence of any elected official who would take the place of the governor, should he die, resign, or otherwise be prevented from fulfilling his official duties. His place is then taken by the secretary of state, an official appointed by the governor and approved by the legislature, as just mentioned. This arrangement has the great advantage over the prevailing practice in American state governments (as well as the Union!) that the temporary successor would be a man thoroughly acquainted with the government's policy, an experienced administrator, and presumably a man of very considerable ability, since the governor must choose him with this possibility in mind. Approval by the legislature presumably means that he also possesses broad political support. But whether such a man would thereafter display the capacity of political party leadership required is an open question. Only experience can tell how this novel arrangement will work over the years.

In any case, the vast appointing power (coupled in the American tradition with the power of removal) gives the governor uncontested hierarchical control of the administration. Indeed, the government of Puerto Rico is probably the most unqualifiedly monolithic and centralized administration under the American flag. It corresponds, as has been repeatedly pointed out, to the blueprint of public administration theorists. Nor is this surprising, considering that teams of public administration experts have been actively engaged in helping to reshape the situation. In the early forties, the heritage of colonial rule had left a great deal of administrative fragmentation and confusion. In the course of the twelve years from 1941 to 1953, this was replaced by a pattern of central control, unprecedented in the annals of American government. But whether such radical centralization of control is an unmixed blessing remains to be seen. Unique circumstances, such as the vigorous party leadership of Muñoz Marín, the homogeneity of the island's population, and the tradition of accepting personal leadership (*personalismo*) have contributed to the success of this pattern so far. Whether they will continue to do so is impossible to say, but while it lasts, it certainly constitutes another unique feature of the island's government. As has been said: "In a relatively short time the reorganization effort has effected changes in the structure and functioning of the executive branch which are unparalleled elsewhere under the American flag." [34]

The very success of these efforts at reform on the island-wide level of state government has obscured what would appear from the standpoint of democratic theory and experience to be the greatest weakness of Puerto Rican government, and that is the way in which local government is conducted. All kinds of activities which, not only in America, but wherever democracy

is practiced, are left to local authorities, are in Puerto Rico
handled by the central government. Not only does this practice
burden the Puerto Rican legislature with a great many local
problems which instead of being carefully considered are sum-
marily dismissed on a log-rolling basis, but local government
is not available as a school in democracy. Indeed, some of the
weakness of the opposition which Muñoz Marín laments is very
probably the result of this failure to provide for home rule.
Under the constitution, local communities are completely at
the mercy of the central legislature. None of their authority is
constitutionally protected. There is a strange paradox involved
here. The insistent demand for self-government vis-à-vis the
federal government has not resulted in an appreciation of the
importance of self-government for the local communities; in
other words, the deeper reasons for self-rule in a plural democratic society have not been fully grasped. It is unquestionably
a decided weakness, but one which can be remedied, because of
the broad power of the legislature. A significant begininng has
recently been initiated in this field.[35] It is, of course, true that
in terms of efficiency and effective service to the people, the
Commonwealth government is superior. No doubt the controller
is right in feeling that "it would not be advisable to transfer
most of the programs and functions now entrusted to the central government to the municipalities." [36] But surely, it would
not be necessary to transfer "most" of the services; some services
of vital local concern would be an important beginning, and as
the controller himself states: "through a gradual process, they
should be granted . . . a broader revenue base, more active
participation in programs now entrusted to the central government, like education and libraries, parks and recreation, planning and utility services." [37] Admittedly, in view of the density
of population and the good roads and adequate lines of com-
munication, great centralization is feasible. But is this reason

enough for having the Commonwealth government supply such essentially local services as fire stations, recreational centers, and public health units, not to speak of schools and water? It would certainly seem true that "the municipalities could very well assume the initiative in providing more adult and preschool education; in supplying running water to rural communities; in expanding recreational facilities; and in participating more actively in local planning and zoning and in slum clearance and new housing." [38] But are they likely to do it as long as primary responsibility in these fields of work is not theirs? Where is the initiative to come from? A radical reversal of the habits of the past is called for, not merely wishful thinking in terms of a gradual approach for which there is not any basis in terms of governmental responsibility and power. Having shown extraordinary inventiveness and resourcefulness in other fields, it is hard to believe that the leaders of Puerto Rico could not solve this vital problem. It has been done in Germany and Italy. So why not here? [39] A very significant beginning has been made in laying the foundations for a radical reversal of the ancient Spanish tradition of centralized administration by the establishment of what is called Community Education.[40]

But, we are told, all this is romanticism. That when faced with a people so poor as the Puerto Ricans and a task as gigantic as the economic development of an island so limited in natural resources, nothing short of central planning and administration will do. This weighty argument brings us face to face with one of the most remarkable features of Puerto Rico, another unique achievement, namely its set-up for democratic planning.[41] There are many who believe that planning is incompatible with democracy.[42] To be sure, planning in a democratic context must be differently conceived from planning under an autocratic rule. Democratic planning, dedicated as it must be to achieving the greatest satisfaction for as many as possible, cannot afford to neglect the reactions of all those whom the policies involved in a plan are likely to affect. Generally speaking, the procedures applicable to sound budgeting are applicable to democratic planning. In keeping with this fact, the Commonwealth has instituted a regular planning program, administered by the Planning Board in the governor's office which operates in close liaison with the Budget Bureau. The Planning Board, besides developing a master plan—it is actually a set of plans each dealing with a particular aspect of the development of the island—submits each year to the legislature a six-year financial program. As Sr. Don Rafael Picó, the first chairman of the Board, has written: "The financial program offers a picture of the island resources and expenditures projected for the following six years. . . . The program is revised annually in order to take into consideration changes in the insular fiscal picture and the development of specific programs." [43]

Besides this fiscal program, the Board is developing and continually adjusting the "guide lines" of economic development in terms of the emergent public needs and interests.[44] Puerto Rico, though a severely underdeveloped land, has provided a really effective setting for the application of such an imaginative approach to the problems of economic development, once broadly and firmly based popular leadership was at hand.

When the fabled Baron Munchhausen told his tall tale of how he had lifted himself from a swamp by his own bootstraps, not many believed him. Unbelievable like his, is the story of Puerto Rico's economic development since 1941, or perhaps better since 1945—for the war years, while profoundly affecting the Puerto Rican economy, did not really provide an opportunity for the comprehensive industrialization which has been Puerto Rico's signal achievement since the end of the war. People talk about the "miracle" of German economic reconstruction, and it is a striking story. But its figures pale, when compared with what has been done in Puerto Rico during the same period. To be sure, this progress may to a considerable extent have been facilitated by the prosperity in the mainland. A prolonged labor shortage, combined with abundant capital, made Puerto Rico unusually attractive to American mainland industries looking for expansion. Unlike the Germans who had their vast industrial know-how to work with, and their industrial labor force to build on, the Puerto Rican economy had to be built from scratch. If one rereads now one of the books that were written in the twenties and thirties, what is said there about the Puerto Rican economy sounds like the description of a totally different country. It is a country where according to these reports over 90 per cent of the population lived from agriculture, where the annual per capita income was around $100.00, where disease was rampant, and where the prospect of feeding the increasing population seemed dismal indeed.[45]

Today, Puerto Rico has surpassed all Latin American countries except Venezuela in per capita income ($445.00 in 1956). Its net national income was just over a billion dollars in 1956, as contrasted with 189 million dollars in 1930.[46] Even allowing for the devaluation of the dollar, this is a unique showing. Income has been rising at the rate of about 2.2 per cent a year. The population has remained stable, for the last three years, due to the unprecedented absorption of as many as 61,000 Puerto Ricans (1956) into the continental United States. The story of how it has been done is one of the most extraordinary ones in the history of industrial capitalism.

In some ways the present popular rulers of Puerto Rico are worthy successors to such men as the Cecils in England and Colbert in France. What would seem even more appropriate a parallel is the vision of Alexander Hamilton at the time of the founding of the Republic.[47] Indeed, in contrast to these representatives of authoritarian and conservative governmental philosophies, the promoters of Puerto Rico today are, of course, part of a markedly more democratic outlook. If bureaucratic and authoritarian tendencies and impulses crop up from time to time, it should be remembered that this is a problem faced by all advanced industrial societies, notably the United States, Great Britain, and France.[48] In terms of the democratic planning process adopted by Puerto Rico, a comparison of the successive six-year fiscal programs reveals that goals have not necessarily been achieved, but have at times been exceeded as well. No trend is distinguishable. If one turns from these programs to the longer-range projections and analyzes the targets for 1955 and 1960,[49] some interesting divergencies appear. To start with, the growth of the population was considerably overestimated. Whereas a net annual increase of 1.4 per cent was assumed, the population rose only by 9,000 during 1956; hence the total (estimated) in 1956 had reached only 2,257,000, as against 2,219,000 in 1950; it had been expected to be 2,380,000 by 1955. A very large emigration to the continental United States and the related decline in the birth-rate were responsible for this divergence. The difference in available labor force was correspondingly striking. As against an expected 845,000 by 1955, there were about 640,000 in 1956. Those who are employed, however, are more fully employed, and receive much better wages. Yet, in spite of this striking drop in total number of workers—there is, e.g., the special situation of the needle workers who have dropped to a fraction of their former number —unemployment did not fall to 9 per cent in 1955, as hoped for, but remained at 13 per cent (1957) which is even a slight increase over the 12.8 per cent of 1950. Yet, the net income increased nearly as sharply as had been planned and reached, as already mentioned, a billion dollars in 1956; the projection had been $1,170.00 in 1955, and roughly $1,320.00 by 1956. The net per capita was to reach $494.00 in 1955 and approximately

$540.00 in 1956; it actually amounted to $445.00, or almost 100 dollars less than planned. In view of the fact that the per capita income still lags greatly behind general U.S. standards—it was just under $1,500.00 for the country as a whole and $873.00 for the poorest state, Mississippi—the rise in per capita income, while gratifying, still has a long way to go, before it catches up.[50]

To these figures of growth in income corresponds, of course, the rate of industrialization. In 1956, the percentage of national income derived from industry for the first time exceeded that derived from agriculture. In a significant review made early in 1958, the governor was able to point out that the number of factories had passed 500, and that the number was increasing rapidly, in spite of the slump on the mainland, with 168 million dollars spent for construction, that reinvestment absorbed 17 per cent of the value of the national production, and that productivity per work hour and consequent take-home-pay continued to rise.* At the same time, he called attention to the fact that very substantial increases in public services will be required, in order to make continued progress at this rate possible. Better harbor facilities and water supply, more electrical energy (a serious setback occurred the previous year in the oil refining field, because of irregularities in electrical energy supply), public health and housing—these and many others will have to be pushed. In asking for public investment of 35 million dollars, he forecast that actually about 60 million dollars on the average will have to be invested annually, if the goals for 1975 are to be achieved. This may mean a public debt by 1975, of 500 million dollars, according to the estimates of the planning board. In the face of this situation, the governor suggested three possibilities: either raise the debt limit very ma-

---

* Whether these trends would persist, if we had a protracted recession or worse in the United States mainland may be doubted.

terially, and place the entire burden of this expansion on future generations, *or* accept the responsibility for a substantial part of these expenditures by paying substantially larger taxes, *or* sacrifice the opportunity of achieving an adequate standard of living for the living generation of Puerto Ricans because at the present rate it cannot be achieved in this century.[51] It is clear that the government favors the second of these alternatives, and is prepared to hasten the rate of capital accumulation by suitable forms of taxation.

Since it is widely believed in the United States that Puerto Rico receives very large federal subsidies, it may be interesting to make some comparison. At the outset, it should be made clear that some of these compilations, popular inside Congress and out, are very misleading. Expenditures of the federal government for federal services, such as the military, the postal service, and the like, ought not to be included; they are not included in the mainland either. They are normally expenditures for value received: the service of Puerto Ricans in the American military forces, the postal fees paid by Puerto Ricans, and so forth. Only grants-in-aid (and a few minor items in education and agriculture primarily) should be included. These run to about 22 million dollars this year, or about $10.00 per capita. Many states in the Union receive very much larger grants-in-aid; Nevada $44.34 and Wyoming even $52.35. To be sure, a federal income tax is levied in these states, but their level of income per capita is so much higher than in Puerto Rico that the difference far exceeds the tax. For example, take Wyoming with its large federal grants. Here the per capita income in 1955 was $1,753.00, while the per capita contribution to the federal treasury was about $195.00, or only about one sixth of the difference in per capita income! The situation for the poorest state, Mississippi, is similar.[52] It can be seen from even these few figures that what the people of a state contribute to the federal treasury and what they receive under various federal programs should in turn be related to their relative state of wealth. Puerto Rico should be seen as an emergency situation, calling for special measures, until the standard of living reaches mainland levels.[53]

The governor has also been stressing the fact that in the long run, continued industrialization and hence economic development will depend upon the success of Puerto Rican education, primary, secondary, and advanced. Here remarkable strides have been made, and yet a great deal remains to be done. While illiteracy is definitely on the way out, the rate dropping rapidly from year to year, a great many people who are no longer illiterate in the technical sense, receive only a few or even only one year of education. It is a matter not only of inadequate plant and equipment, including even elementary school buildings, but also and more importantly perhaps, a matter of teachers. Great progress will have to be achieved, both quantitatively and qualitatively, if the goal of a bilingual industrial population is to be realized. The danger of bilingualism sinking to the level of "double semilingualism," as Muñoz Marín has dubbed it, should be avoided as far as possible. That it can be done, the example of Switzerland shows. But it requires a very special effort, which well-to-do Switzerland can more readily afford than poor Puerto Rico.[54]

I should like to add that as the educational system of Puerto Rico matures, and as local government gains strength and vigor, one must hope that educational responsibility will become more decentralized. In the long run, such decentralization has proved highly beneficial. No doubt, the stimulus of a highly centralized effort was needed at the outset. But there is such a need of continuous, active participation and interest of the parents and of the local community of which they form a part, that Puerto Rico will want to extend local responsibilities in the years ahead. One does not need to go the length North America has gone in order to appreciate the value of local interest and initiative in this field of work, so vital to both the economy and culture, as well as the government of a free society.

In conclusion, I hope I may be considered justified in repeating that in the economic, governmental, and political sphere remarkable, indeed unique achievements are the manifestations of Puerto Rico's new won freedom and autonomy. We have only mentioned some of them; quite a few others had to be left aside. In the last chapter, there will be some further hints. But there can be no question that freedom has amply rewarded the men who struggled to achieve it.

NOTES

1. See for a comparative survey *Studies in Federalism* (I, 10) and K. C. Wheare's *Federal Government* (1945; 3rd. ed., 1953), *passim*. The first of these contains extensive references to the workings of American federalism, including a chapter on overseas territories (XIV) and on new states (XV).

2. Quoted by Rexford G. Tugwell in his statement before the Senate Committee on Territories and Insular Affairs, in February, 1943, which is reprinted in Tugwell's *Puerto Rican Public Papers* (1945), pp. 146 ff. He commented quite justly that "the people of Puerto Rico accepted this as a kind of contract and waited for its fulfillment."

3. For a general history of Puerto Rico, see Salvador Brau, *Historia de Puerto Rico* (New York, 1904); rather elementary. Cf. also the *Boletines Históricos de Puerto Rico* (since 1914) and the sketch in K. Mixer, *Porto Rico* (1926). A good analysis of the autonomy statute (*Carta Autonomica*) is briefly, but ably discussed by Pedro Muñoz-Amato in "Major Trends in the Constitutional History of Puerto Rico—1493–1917," *Rivista de Derecho, Legislación v. Jurisprudencia* (1951), pp. 251 ff. The text is found in *Documents on the Constitutional History of Puerto Rico* (no date), pp. 22 ff.

4. See Rexford G. Tugwell, *The Stricken Land* (1947). Cf. also his reappraisal some five years later "What next for Puerto Rico!" in *Annals* (I, 11), pp. 145 ff. Here he goes so far as to say: "Puerto

Rico, I think, is likely to become a state." See also R. G. Tugwell, *Puerto Rican Public Papers* (1945).

5. This remark, often repeated by the governor in his conversations, is by Hanson, *op. cit.*, attributed to an interlocutor at one of the election meetings of Muñoz Marín. I doubt that he did more than echo what was a basic element in the new approach of the *Populares:* to relegate the status problem to second place, and to put the economic development and social betterment of the island first. It continues to be their view. A striking instance of early overconfidence is the pamphlet by Bolívar Pagan, the resident commissioner, *Puerto Rico—The Next State* (1924).

6. See Rexford G. Tugwell, *Puerto Rican Public Papers* (1945), pp. 181 ff and 486 ff. For the emotional and political background, compare his work cited above, note 4, p. 335, and some of the preceding pages as well as the whole chapter of which this passage is the beginning. The Committee set up by Roosevelt at the time and described by Tugwell is considered by some to have been of decisive importance. See p. 492 where the beginnings of the commonwealth concept are hinted at.

7. *Documents*, as quoted in note 2, pp. 163 ff. It was done in the form of an amendment to the Organic Act of 1917 (Jones Act) which replaced the Foraker Act (May 1, 1900). *Ibid.*, pp. 64 ff (Foraker). The Jones Act is found on pp. 81 ff.

8. The foregoing provisions are found in Sec. 5, 2, 25 ff, and 36; see *Laws of Puerto Rico Annotated* (1954), pp. 49 ff.

9. Even Tugwell who had no desire to thwart the popular will found it necessary to veto many bills which, as he says, *op. cit.*, note 4, seem to have been put forward in the knowledge that they would be vetoed. Cf. also Henry Wells, "The Legislative Assembly: Powers and Procedures," in *Readings on the Government of Puerto Rico* (1956—mimeographed for the College of Social Sciences of the University of Puerto Rico), pp. 94–95: "Out of narrowly partisan or demagogic motives the legislative majority often passed bad legislation, secure in the knowledge that the governor would veto it."

10. Tugwell, *op. cit.*, note 4, pp. 83–84.

11. For the theory of the constituent group and its power see *Constitutional Government and Democracy* (1950), chs. VII and VIII and the references given there.

12. See Art. IV, sec. 3: "The Congress shall have power to dispose of and make all needful rules and regulations respecting the territory or other property belonging to the United States. . . ." Although both governmental practice and judicial interpretation has largely ignored it, the language does not seem to justify the rule over persons at all, as the article speaks only of territory in the singular, and relates it to "other property." No power over citizens of the United States in their personal relations was evidently thought of. A consultation of the Debates leads to a similar conclusion.

13. See David M. Helfeld, "Congressional Intent and Attitude toward Public Law 600 and the Constitution of the Commonwealth of Puerto Rico," *Rivista Jurídica de la Universidad de Puerto Rico,* XXI (1952), pp. 225 ff.

14. We do not until now have a detailed study of this process, but it is hoped that one will soon be made. In the meantime, the following articles may be consulted: Henry Wells, "Constitutional Development in Puerto Rico" in *Developments Toward Self-Government in the Caribbean* (1954); A. Morales Carrión, "The Commonwealth of Puerto Rico—Its Historical Roots and Present Significance," Eighth Annual Conference on the Caribbean, University of Florida; Gordon K. Lewis, "Puerto Rico: A New Constitution in American Government," *The Journal of Politics,* XV (1953), pp. 42 ff.; Antonio Fernós-Isern, "From Colony to Commonwealth," *The Annals,* January, 1953, pp. 16 ff.; C. J. Friedrich, "Considérations générales sur la constitution de Porto-Rico," in *Revue Internationale d'Histoire Politique et Constitutionnelle,* July–October, 1951; and Peter Fliess, "Puerto Rico's Political Status under the New Constitution," *The Western Political Quarterly,* V (1952), pp. 635 ff. See also the materials prepared for the Convention *La Nueva Constitución de Puerto Rico* (1954).

15. See the comments by Pedro Muñoz-Amato in "Congressional Conservatism and the Commonwealth Relationship," *Annals* (I, 11) pp. 27–31. See also, *Laws of Puerto Rico Annotated,* pp. 125 ff. (on the establishment of the Commonwealth) and pp. 157 ff. (on the Federal Relations Act).

16. For a review of these cases, see Calvert Magruder, "The Commonwealth Status of Puerto Rico," in *University of Pittsburgh Law Review,* XV (1953), p. 1 ff.

17. *Downes v. Bidwell,* 182 US 244 (1901); cf. also *De Lima v. Bidwell,* 182 US 1 (1901).

18. See Ivor Jennings, *Parliament* (1940). Magruder, *loc. cit.,* gives a number of instances in which future Congresses are limited by the creation of vested rights (p. 14) and how this might apply to Puerto Rico, without stating a firm conclusion.

19. Mentioned by Magruder, *loc. cit.,* p. 14.

20. Concerning the doctrine *rebus sic stantibus,* see the skillfully balanced discussion in Wesley L. Gould, *An Introduction to International Law* (1957), pp. 339–345 and the literature cited there, especially Scelle, Lauterpacht, Kelson, Kaufmann, and Nussbaum.

21. E. B. Greene, *The Provincial Governor in the English Colonies of North America* (1898).

22. See Charles E. Clark and William D. Rogers, "The New Judiciary Act of Puerto Rico: A Definitive Court Reorganization," *Yale Law Review,* LXI (1952), pp. 1147 ff.

23. State, Justice, Education, Health, Treasury, Labor, Agriculture, and Commerce and Public Works are the eight Departments. They are so given in the constitution, art. IV, sec. 6, but may be changed by the legislature. Cf. Henry Wells, "Administrative Structure of the Commonwealth Government," in *op. cit.,* pp. 150 ff.

24. Wells, *loc. cit.,* p. 36; also p. 84 ff.

25. Wells, *ibid.,* p. 45.

26. Wells, *ibid.,* pp. 53 ff.

27. Wells, *ibid.,* p. 49.

28. Wells, *ibid.,* pp. 79 ff. and pp. 89 ff.

29. Wells, *ibid.,* p. 83.

30. Wells, *ibid.,* pp. 44 ff. See also *Constitution,* Art. III, sec. 4.

31. Wells, *ibid.,* p. 67 and preceding. The next quote is from p. 66.

32. Wells, *ibid.,* pp. 100 ff. offers a good treatment entitled "The Office of the Governor of the Commonwealth of Puerto Rico," first draft, April 2, 1956. I have profited greatly from his analysis.

33. See Henry Wells, "Administrative Reorganization in Puerto Rico," *Western Political Quarterly,* IX (1956), pp. 470–490; note esp. his conclusions at pp. 488 ff.

34. For a sage appraisal, see Wells, *ibid.,* p. 490. Wells also rightly warns against drawing too general conclusions from the Puerto Rican experience. The quotation is found *ibid.,* p. 484.

35. Cf. for this ch. XIII of (II, 11). As we there said: "The violent

upheavals of our time have revived interest in the local community. Its importance for the functioning of constitutional government is common knowledge." Cf. also the views of Dewey, Bryce, and others discussed there.

36. R. de J. Cordero in Wells, *op. cit.* (II, 9), pp. 172 ff.

37. *Ibid.*, p. 174.

38. The difficulties of carrying through on such general hopes and prayers are well illustrated in American metropolitan communities. For further information, see the recent issues of *The Annals*, November, 1957, entitled "Metropolis in Ferment."

39. For the recent development of local government in Germany, see the chapter in Edward H. Litchfield (ed.), *The Government of Post-War Germany* (1954) by Roger Wells: "Local Government," pp. 57–83; for Italy the Communità movement is particularly significant; see for it their journal *Communità* and the programmatic study by Adriano Olivetti, *L'Ordine Politico delle Communità* (1946). For an outline of Puerto Rican local government, see A. G. C. Carmona Romay, *Programa de Gobierno Municipal* (Havana, 1950), who seeks to identify a middle ground between Spanish centralist and Anglo-Saxon localist tradition.

40. A vivid description of this work is given by Hanson, *op. cit.*, ch. XIX. See also above, ch. I, pp. 15–16.

41. See Rafael Picó "The Role of Planning in Puerto Rico," *Annals* (I, 11), pp. 70 ff.

42. See F. A. Hayek, *The Road to Serfdom* (1944), and my review article in *American Political Science Review*, XXIX (1945), pp. 575 ff. The problem is discussed within the broader context of constitutional democracy in the work cited in note 11.

43. Picó, *op. cit.*, pp. 40–41.

44. See *Economic Development of Puerto Rico, 1940–50; 1951–60* (ed. Perloff), published by the Planning Board in 1951. I also was given the privilege of examining the confidential annual planning reports for recent years. It is in this field, more than any other, perhaps, that one can discern the influence of Rexford Tugwell's thinking. Coming to Puerto Rico immediately after having been chairman of the New York City Planning Commission, he inspired a group of younger men with his vision of an effective democratic planning process. Cf. Tugwell's own account, *op. cit.*, note 4.

45. See K. Mixer, *Porto Rico, History and Conditions, Social, Economic and Political* (1926), pp. 120 ff. and *Puerto Rico—A Guide to the Island of Boriquen*, American Guide Series (1940), pp. 73 ff.

46. See Department of the Treasury, *Report on Finances and Economy —1956* (no date).

47. Consult Alexander Hamilton's famous Report on *Manufactures* of 1791, *Works* (ed. by H. C. Lodge, 1885–1886), vol. IV, pp. 70–204. Cf. concerning this F. S. Oliver, *Alexander Hamilton* (new ed., 1925), pp. 228 ff.

48. The problem of bureaucracy is central in all modern government. Cf. my *Constitutional Government and Democracy* (3rd ed., 1950), esp. chs. II and XIX, and the literature cited there. An interesting recent study of the problem in a comparable setting has been published by O. D. Corpuz, *The Bureaucracy in the Philippines*, Institute of Public Administration, University of the Philippines, 1957. The chapter on Spanish colonial administration may apply, to a degree.

49. See especially the Report of the Planning Board entitled *Economic Development—Puerto Rico—1940–1950—1950–1960* (1951), more particularly pp. 89 ff.

50. Figures are taken from the *Statistical Abstract of the United States* (1956). The opinion, often heard, that in view of this situation people might shift their residence to Puerto Rico is not in fact a valid point, for two reasons: (1) the island income tax approximates the federal income tax, so that the gain would not differ materially from that realized by a man moving into a state without state income tax; and (2) federal income tax must be paid on all income earned outside of Puerto Rico.

51. See the *Mesaje* of Luis Muñoz Marín, of January 22, 1958, as printed *in extenso* in *El Mundo*, January 23, 1958, p. 14.

52. Figures again from the *Statistical Abstract of the United States* (1956). It is interesting to note that if federal excise taxes were not recovered into the Puerto Rican Treasury, but contributed to the U.S. Treasury, the contribution would amount to a total of approximately 18 millions, according to the Puerto Rican Treasury, or decidedly less than $10.00 per capita. See *Report on Finances and Economy 1956*, pp. 8–9. It would be interesting to calculate the amount involved in federal income taxes, were they levied in

Puerto Rico. In view of the large number of income earners falling in the exempt categories, this amount ought not to be overestimated.

53. The situation is similar in the case of the Virgin Islands. See my memorandum, as made public by Senator Ottley for the Organic Act Commission in 1957.

54. Cf. the Reports of the Secretary of Education, and the apt summary in Hanson, *op. cit.*, ch. XVIII. In 1951, the operation cost per child was about $62.00, way below U.S. standards. Yet, in 1957 the largest single expenditure, 29 per cent, of the budget of the Commonwealth was for education.

3

A Permanent Solution?

The present is already past. What really belongs
to human beings, is the future.

Bolivár in a letter to Santander, 1820.

THE GREAT STRIDES which Puerto Rico has made in the last
twelve years must not be allowed to obscure the ineluctable
fact that they are part of a transition toward a permanent
solution, and not this solution itself. In the course of our discussions, it has become amply clear, I trust, that and how the present state of affairs falls short of any permanent solution. It remains for us to sketch in broad outline the nature of such a
final state.

I do not believe that there will be much disagreement on
the score of an adequate standard of living, though beyond that
elementary basis, there is apt to be disagreement not only in
political and constitutional terms, but in economic, social, and
cultural respects as well. Now it may well be that those who
argue for either statehood or independence as the *necessary*
final state will turn out to have been right. It may well be that
Puerto Ricans will in due course become so merged in the Anglo-
American culture, through constant migration back and forth,
as well as infiltration of American standards and ways of life,
resulting from the multitude of contacts which the present relationship entails, that eventually nothing but statehood will
seem right. No less an authority than former Governor Tug-

well gave expression to this surmise, when he wrote: "Puerto
Rico, I think, is likely to become a state. I think this is so because no proud and achieving people can go on being excluded
from participation in the highest political processes of the
nation of which it is a part." [1] True enough; but we now see that
such participation can be brought about in other ways than
through statehood. And we believe that the economic tasks
Puerto Rico still faces cannot be solved, if Puerto Rico were to
become one of the states of the Union. By the time they are
solved—simply projecting the present rate of progress and that
means being optimistic, obviously—fifteen to twenty years
will elapse, and it would seem wiser to structure the relationship soundly in the next few years, rather than to await so un-
certain a terminal point.

It is likewise possible that the trend of the last decade might
well be reversed; that Puerto Ricans might want to relinquish
their American citizenship, and no longer want to migrate to
the continental United States but become instead culturally,
economically, and politically, part of a broadly conceived Caribbean federation. One able student of these matters wrote recently: "The Puerto Rican future in the long run will have to
be related to her natural economic environment in the Carib-
bean-Middle American states system as a whole, instead of being
considered within the exclusive framework of the American
commercial system." [2] Maybe so. But the empirical observer
of the Caribbean world is struck by the fact that these islands
and their mainland counterparts have little to give to each
other economically. Their interests are not complementary, but
competitive, and all of them would gain from linkage either
with Europe or with America, even on a permanent basis. In
any case, it would seem unlikely, even though the possibility
should not be excluded, that so radical a reversal of the present
trend in Puerto Rico and of the sentiment of their people would

occur within the next fifteen to twenty years. If not, the same argument applies that has just been stated with regard to the statehood advocates.

But all this reasoning depends upon the fashioning of a more permanent solution. If no such solution were found, surely one of the alternatives would come to the fore within the foreseeable future. Let us then turn to the constituents of this permanent solution. But first a note of caution! Such a permanent solution should not be looked upon as an action program for the day after tomorrow. Stages will have to be envisaged for its accomplishment. The concrete reality of politics and economics does not fit into neat boxes. Puerto Rican and Presidential elections occur at four year intervals. Stalins die at unforeseen moments, and the rate of technological progress seems to be subject to the vagaries suggested by Sputnik and the hydrogen bomb. But without being rigid about the time span involved, let us for the following analysis assume that we are dealing with three stages of which the past ten years are the first one. What will Puerto Rico, as a permanent associated and free state be like in 1975? [3]

The economy should, in the course of the next decade, achieve the kind of productive strength that would be represented by a standard of living not less than that in the poorest state of the continental U.S. today. That may not mean exactly the same money income per capita, because there may be hidden advantages, due to climate, which would provide the same standard of living in Puerto Rico at somewhat lower money cost. Still, it would mean a doubling of the present per capita income, if the population stayed stationary. Since the net national income rose roughly 350 millions between 1950 and 1956 and since about twice the present national income would be required, it is evident that to achieve this goal in ten years would be a remarkable accomplishment. But while it was being accomplished, a different task would have to be tackled, the fulfillment of which would be the consummation of the third stage: stabilizing the economy at this level and achieving the kind of equilibrium which would enable it to absorb from year to year the additional labor becoming available, in other words to provide from national savings enough growth to take care of all Puerto Ricans, rather than allowing them to be siphoned off to the mainland. By then, the per capita income should approximate that of the national average which at present is about $1,500.00. Since income keeps rising, it may be more by then. In any case, at the end of this generation, in 1975 a "permanent" solution would mean a Puerto Rico economically reasonably self-contained as a partner of the American economy. Its population and its national product would be growing at about the same rate as the rest of the U.S. In the course of this transformation Puerto Rico should become able to make an annual contribution to the federal treasury in lieu of federal income taxes. Something like a 10 per cent addition to Puerto Rican income tax collections might be a feasible plan on a permanent basis.

Culturally and socially, Puerto Rico would in the course of these years continue to integrate and develop its distinctively Spanish tradition, with the Spanish language continuing as the dominant idiom, but more generally supplemented by English. It is evident that a people as gifted as the Puerto Ricans ought to be fully capable of such a feat. Not only the French Canadians, but the Swiss, to mention just two outstanding examples, have achieved a bilingual cultural existence, with great benefit to themselves as well as to those with whom they share each of the languages. But this goal of full and effective bilingualism is in a sense merely the outward sign of an inner achievement, that of effectively blending two cultural ingredients, not in a static, but in a dynamic and growing way. And a highly dynamic task it is. For neither North American nor Latin-American culture is going to stand still; they are both undergoing remarkable changes at the present time. The Puerto Ricans will be continually challenged by these innovations, they will be continually called upon to discover the common ground and the creative potential of a genuine encounter. In this respect, the Swiss have been very much more successful than the French Canadians, who only in recent years have begun to grasp the important potential embedded in such an intercultural position as they occupy. I confess to having a sense of extraordinary future achievements in this field which will make the present state of affairs seem rather inadequate. The remarkable growth and development of the University of Puerto Rico has hitherto been tied to the strongly utilitarian requirements of a people desperately struggling for survival. As that survival becomes increasingly assured, and the economy becomes stabilized in the manner just sketched, we may expect a liberation of creative forces among the younger generation which should provide inspiration for both of the cultures in which the Puerto Ricans are destined to participate. Activities such as the Casals Music Festival which patently constitutes an impressive projection of Puerto Rico's musical tradition will have multiplied. Indeed I expect the University of Puerto Rico to have become a leading American university.

But economic and cultural activities, basic as they are, depend upon what framework is provided by the political order. Aristotle's challenge that the science of what is required in this field is the master science, still holds true. It is here that man's nature is most nearly free, where man fashions his own destiny to a larger extent than anywhere else. It is in the sphere of government and politics that innovation bears the richest fruit, if it provides the space for living beings to unfold and come to fruition. I shall therefore give more detailed attention to this sphere of political action. As we said already, a failure to define and develop the present alternative of a commonwealth status, placing it upon a firm and permanent basis, might mean either independence, statehood, or a relapse into a semicolonial status. In 1940, the Popular Party inclined to believe that the status question could be sidestepped, and the economic development be made the primary concern. Events soon showed that economic development continually raised problems of a political order. It has been the same in more recent years. The imperfections of the present federal relations set-up have handicapped the culture and economy of the island to some extent.

At an earlier point in our analysis we spoke of five shortcomings in the present federal relations. Let me repeat them now. There is first the failure to provide for active Puerto Rican participation in the process of federal legislation (including constitutional amendments). There is second the failure to provide for participation in the shaping of foreign and defense policies. There is third the failure to envisage a contribution of Puerto Rico to the federal treasury. There is fourth the failure to give Puerto Rico the same freedom as other states regarding a number of clearly local matters, such as citizenship and the debt. There is finally the failure to enable the people of Puerto Rico to develop its own bill of rights, as long as they do so within the provisions of the Constitution. To these may be added, as a corollary of the first, the problem of how to associate the government of Puerto Rico with the execution of those laws which are made applicable to Puerto Rico.

Before we turn to these specific issues, one general remark is in order. Plans for the permanent status of Puerto Rico should, if at all possible, avoid the necessity of amending the American Constitution. In the first place, it is a well-known fact that the process of amending the Constitution is very cumbersome and that usually many years elapse, before an amendment is ratified.

Many more attempts have failed than succeeded, because it is a formidable task to educate a majority of over 160 million people to the point where they will support a policy in an unfamiliar field. In the case of Puerto Rico, it would mean that during the entire intervening period tensions and mutual recriminations would poison the relationship between the Commonwealth and the rest of America. Nor is it readily to be seen where the people of Puerto Rico are to find the means for carrying on the far-flung campaign of public education and propaganda that would be required. We shall therefore try to develop the permanent status within the four corners of the existing Constitution, broadly interpreted, with one exception.

With these thoughts in mind, let us see what Puerto Rican federal relations may be like in 1975. Puerto Ricans will, by then, have achieved a substantial amount of participation in applicable federal legislation. Such participation will go considerably beyond what the resident commissioner is able to do today, though that is not inconsiderable; but it is indirect participation at best. What a change! A thoughtful student was able to, in 1955, describe Puerto Rico's position vis-à-vis the Congress as "in many ways still governed by Congressional committees." [4] That may have been something of an exaggeration, but there was enough truth in it, to serve as an uncomfortable reminder. Complete Puerto Rican autonomy regarding her own constitution will, of course, have become guaranteed explicitly in the Federal Relations Act. That act itself will, in keeping with its nature—in the nature of a compact!—have become incontestably unalterable, except with Puerto Rican assent. But what is more, Puerto Rican consent will have become a necessary requirement for all applicable federal legislation. Congress made this very broad additional concession, because it had become widely recognized inside Congress and out that such participation flows from the principle of self-government which is ac-

knowledged as the basis of the entire settlement. Self-government means government not only by consent, but by participation in the process of legislation. This has been a generally
acknowledged doctrine in the English-speaking world since
the days of John Locke. It was acknowledged both in the Declaration of Independence and in the Constitution.[5] The people
of Puerto Rico do not participate in either the election of Congress or of the President, and hence federal legislation is at present adopted without the active and formal participation of the
Puerto Rican people or their representatives. Since federal legislation covers much of the life of every American citizen it may
be argued—and it was so argued before the United Nations [6]—
that Puerto Rico is non-self-governing and merely possesses
some measure of local home-rule, like a number of British
colonies. To this charge, the answer may be given that since
the resident commissioner is elected by the people and since the
Congress has shown considerable inclination to exempt the
commonwealth from the application of laws to which the
Puerto Ricans object, as well as allowing for their objections in
framing applicable laws, there is in fact participation by the
people of Puerto Rico in federal legislation. One might add that
the people of many a state in the Union also find themselves
overruled time and again on laws which they do not like. Fur-
thermore, there is no discrimination against Puerto Ricans as
such. A Puerto Rican resident on the mainland will, of course,
participate in elections and therefore in legislation,[7] while a
mainlander settling in Puerto Rico will not. These facts seem to
me to prove the untenability of the present arrangements, rather
than the opposite.

The answer in my opinion lies in the direction in which
actual legislative custom has already been heading. The applicability of federal legislation to Puerto Rico should be subject to
consideration and formal assent by the Puerto Rican legislative

authorities, i.e., the legislature and the governor. This purpose can be accomplished in a number of ways. The legislature of Puerto Rico may be given the right to declare any law "inapplicable," or it may be given the right to request the suspension of any law that has been made applicable, subject to further negotiations, either between the President and the governor, or in some other manner. The more far-reaching suggestion that no law become applicable, unless approved, would probably mean an unmanageable burden for the Puerto Rican legislature which would have to follow all federal legislation closely. Whereas their right to declare any law "inapplicable" would not lead to such declarations, in most cases, but would enable the resident commissioner to negotiate the "applicability" with a much firmer hand than heretofore.[8] However it is done and whichever of these alternatives is adopted, it is probably necessary at the outset, for reasons of expediency and in order to establish the principle of the matter, to exclude from its reach the fields of foreign relations and defense, as well as that of federal fiscal legislation and more especially the budget and other appropriations acts. The latter could be justified by Puerto Rico's special fiscal status as far as revenue legislation is concerned. However, such concessions can only be temporary. They raise squarely the issue as to what is involved in the permanent solution.

But even if by 1975, all applicable federal legislation had been accepted by Puerto Rico, through active participation, I believe that another change might well have been brought about to implement this legislative work. For it is part of the concept of association that the Puerto Rican people do not participate in the election of the President, nor could they without a constitutional amendment. For this reason, the administration of applicable federal laws may well have been placed in their own hands by that time, under federal supervision. This would not be as unheard-of an arrangement, as might be imagined. Switzerland, with its multicultural and multilingual population, has long practiced this art of "delegated administration" [9] and it has worked well. To be sure, in the United States by contrast, it has been customary to have federal laws executed by federal administrations, and state laws by state officials, although there have been some recent experiments with delegation.[10] The traditional American practice has tended to enhance the position of the federal authorities. In some fields, such as foreign policy and defense, the federal administration is of course unavoidable, and is accepted even in Switzerland. But in many other fields, federal laws could well be executed by state bodies. It provides greater local autonomy to arrange matters that way. Where linguistic and other cultural factors are important, the daily contact of the government with the people ought to be carried on by men of their own culture. I believe that it would be an important part of a permanent solution. So I trust that the year 1975 will find few, if any, federal officials in Puerto Rico. There might be those who would be apprehensive, lest the federal supervision of such state execution of federal laws might smack of colonialism. But if the tried practices of Switzerland are followed, this possibility would not exist. For one, most supervisory activity might be carried out in writing and channeled through the Governor's office.

The status of an associated free commonwealth obviously is a type of federal relationship that is more loose than that of a regular state within the Union. For most Americans, citizens of states of the Union, participation in foreign affairs works through several primary channels. First, the senators participate in the ratification of treaties, second, the House of Representatives has a primary say, where appropriations are involved, and third, both houses, but more particularly the Senate, are currently informed of developments in foreign policy. We might add that citizens of various states, in the course of the regular workings of party activity, are chosen to represent the United States in various international agencies and the like. But overshadowing all, there is, of course, the citizen's share in electing the President who is primarily responsible for the nation's foreign affairs.

It is clear that the status of a free and associated commonwealth calls for delicate adjustments of all this machinery, if direct participation in federal elections which under the Constitution is only provided for citizens of regular states (and hence would require a constitutional amendment), is to remain outside our consideration. To take up treaties first, it presumably should be possible to provide for the nonapplicability formula in this field. I am not minimizing the far-reaching implications of this proposition. To give to the people of Puerto Rico and their representatives the right to refuse their consent to any treaty the United States may enter into, thereby making it inapplicable to the island, is to encounter opposition. Such an arrangement involves the most hotly contested aspect of the Bricker amendment. Yet, I insist that eventually one of two alternatives is essential to a final solution. *Either*, the specific consent to the applicability of treaties to Puerto Rico should be required. This could take the form of making the applicability of implementing legislation subject to the assent of the Puerto Rican legislative authorities, thereby avoiding certain difficulties of international law. *Or*, the resident commissioner could be given a vote in the Senate, whenever treaty decisions were to be taken. But could this be done without a constitutional amendment? It would seem more than doubtful.

As for legislative participation in the shaping of foreign policy, it would seem that the resident commissioner should become a member of the Foreign Relations Committee of both houses, as of right. There is, of course, a good deal of disagreement as to what congressional participation in foreign policy amounts to. But whatever the range, it is clear that the views of Puerto Rico should be fully shared by members of the Congress and that they should play their part in shaping American foreign policy, especially in regard to the Caribbean and Latin America.

In view of the President's role in foreign policy, I believe that the role of Puerto Rico should be even more broadly defined. I believe that the President, as well as the Secretary of State, should periodically review with the governor of Puerto Rico the entire foreign policy of the United States, with special reference to the Caribbean and Latin America, so as to enable the chief executive of Puerto Rico to contribute from his own special vantage point to the effective shaping of American foreign policy. Such periodical meetings would, in a way, correspond to the meetings of Dominion Prime Ministers which Great Britain has developed in recent years as an important link within the Commonwealth of Nations. Since the tie between the Dominions and Britain is admittedly much less close than that between the U.S. and Puerto Rico, the case for such participation is a strong one. A stipulation to this effect in the Federal Relations Act, though not essential perhaps, would be highly desirable.

Finally, there is the problem of representation in international bodies. Should Puerto Rico on a permanent basis be separately represented in various bodies, such as the International Labor Office or UNESCO? There is, of course, no reason why Puerto Ricans, like all other Americans, ought not to represent the United States in such bodies, especially when their unique position vis-à-vis the culture of Latin America would provide them with special knowledge and skills. On the other hand, would it be compatible with the common citizenship to have Puerto Rico carry on a separate policy which might be at variance with that of the United States? For if it were never that, what would be the use of separate representation? Prior consultation and effective cooperation with the State Department and other U.S. agencies seems so essential that it might well be argued that separate and independent representation is incompatible with the status of a free and associated commonwealth. Still, there is the precedent of Great Britain and the Commonwealth, where a common citizenship is not thought to be incompatible with separate foreign policies. If the matter could be worked out in such a way that the arrangement would not imperil the bonds of mutual affection and regard between Puerto Rico and the rest of the United States, it might be feasible. At present, it would seem better to strengthen effective participation of Puerto Rico in American foreign policy, as outlined above. At the same time, there is no reason why the Commonwealth might not be represented at nonpolitical organizations, boards, and conferences which are multiplying in the international field today.

Closely related to the sphere of foreign relations is that of defense. Governmental power has always been based upon the ability to provide effective defense and reasonable security. As long as Puerto Rico is part of the United States, it will and must be defended. Indeed, Puerto Rico is the location of important installations of the United States' military, naval, and air defense system which guard the approaches to the Panama canal, and maintain the U.S. position in the Caribbean. The strategy of nuclear war may have reduced their importance somewhat, but it remains significant. There is a certain mutual interest involved here!

This mutuality of interest in the common defense brings with it a sharing of the burdens, both financial and human. At the present time, Puerto Rico shares only in the human burden: her sons and daughters are as liable to military service

as all other Americans. Could it be otherwise? The proudest
claim of any citizen of a free country is to participate in its
defense. Since the ancients, citizenship and the duty to bear
arms have been closely linked. Machiavelli attributed the decline
of republics to the refusal of the citizen to bear arms in its defense, as happened in Rome. In the heyday of Greek ascendancy,
only slaves and helots did not serve in the defense of Athens and
Sparta. In any final solution, Puerto Ricans will want to share
this "right to bear arms." [11]

But if this is so, then a final solution calls for a reappraisal
of the present lack of any effective participation of Puerto
Ricans in the shaping of defense policies for the United States,
crucial as they are for their own survival. The justification offered at present for such lack of participation, namely that
Puerto Rico makes no contribution to the federal treasury, will
no longer exist in the final solution here delineated. Conse-
quently, in a permanent commonwealth relationship, federal defense legislation should be subject to similar rules concerning
applicability as is other legislation. In order to avoid any challenge to this principle on the ground that it would give Puerto
Rico the right to reject military service it ought to be met
by embodying in the "compact" (Federal Relations Act) a
provision stating that the citizens of Puerto Rico shall serve in
the armed forces of the United States, and that the United
States is committed to the defense of Puerto Rico, thus render-
ing the matter one of mutual agreement. For the rest, a con-
sultative procedure between the President and Puerto Rico's
chief executive, similar to the arrangement suggested for foreign affairs, would compensate in a measure for the fact that
Puerto Ricans do not participate in the election of their Com-
mander-in-Chief. By such a pattern of indirect participation
in defense policy and execution, the rights of the citizens of
Puerto Rico would be preserved, and any implication that

Puerto Ricans are second-class citizens who do not share in the defense of their country as a matter of right would be removed.

The fact that Puerto Rico does not at present, contribute to the federal treasury, but derives substantial financial benefits from it under federal statutes, is politically highly undesirable, while economically being absolutely essential.[12] As mentioned earlier in this chapter, the Puerto Rican economy should, as part of a permanent solution, be able to bear the burden of an annual contribution to the federal treasury.

It is typical for the more flexible status of association that it would be a "contribution" from the state to the federal treasury, rather than taxes levied by the federal union itself. This arrangement prevails in the case of the United Nations; it was also thus planned for the European political community. That does not mean that Puerto Rico might not, on its own authority, tie such a contribution to the income tax. If this were to be 10 per cent of the island income taxes collected, it would at the present moment amount to about four million dollars; if the per capita income doubled, as envisaged above, it might be between eight and ten million. Since federal grant-in-aid programs of one kind or another bring about twenty million dollars to Puerto Rico, someone might say: what is the use of it? Just reduce the federal contribution to the Puerto Rican economy. But such an argument would be highly artificial. All the poorer states of the Union receive substantially more than they contribute. In any case, the argument overlooks that grants-in-aid are part of *federal* policy determination, while the contribution to the federal treasury would presumably be part of the compact. It may be fixed for long periods of time, and usually has been. In short, what the people of a state contribute to the federal treasury and what they receive under various federal programs embodying economic and social policy for the United

States are two quite distinct matters. Let us say, therefore, that by 1975 Puerto Rico would be contributing between five and ten million dollars to the federal treasury.

One of the special problems, mentioned above, is that of the Puerto Rican debt. The present limit embodied in the Federal Relations Act is, of course, a colonial anachronism. By 1975, this will have been replaced by a provision in the Puerto Rican constitution, fixing the debt limit in relation to island tax resources, and the federal government will have no more concern with it than it has with other state debts. Under such an arrangement, there will have occurred a substantial increase in the Puerto Rican debt, but this increase will be soundly related to its economic growth so that Puerto Rico's good financial standing will be unimpaired.

There is one other fiscal problem to be considered in connection with a permanent solution. It springs from the fact that the federal budget has become the focal point of such economic planning as is compatible with a free and democratic constitutional order. Since Puerto Rico has, as we have seen, a very forward looking approach to the task of democratic planning, and since federal and state fiscal policy and planning interact, a link of the two would be an important part of a permanent solution. How could the Puerto Rican government participate in the federal process of financial policy making? I believe that in addition to such special cooperation as may be worked out by the resident commissioner in collaborating with the respective committees on Congress, standing committees should link the two bureaus of the budget and the planning office with the Council of Economic Advisers. Whether such an arrangement ought to apply to regular states as well, it would seem an essential part of a permanent solution.

We turn finally to certain complex problems of the constitutional order as such. There are two sides to this fundamental right of Puerto Ricans to participate in the shaping of their basic law: the federal Constitution and their own constitution. These raise distinct issues which call for settlement in a permanent solution. In discussing the problem of federal legislation in its application to Puerto Rico and what is needed here, we did not consider constitutional amendments. The constitution of Puerto Rico acknowledges [13] that it must remain in accord with the federal Constitution by providing that all Puerto Rican constitutional amendments (and of course, laws) shall be "consistent with the *applicable* provisions of the Constitution of the United States," (italics supplied). This provision raises some very difficult issues. For what are the applicable provisions? [14] And which provisions have under the compact become "inapplicable"? The answer to these questions surely ought to be spelled out specifically in the Federal Relations Act. But there is an even more perplexing question: what about future amendments to the Constitution? If the present Constitution were part of the compact, as indeed it is, how could changes in it be justified without the consent of both parties to the compact? One might argue that in accepting the Constitution as a framework, the Puerto Rican people had also accepted its known methods of amendment, and formally this is true enough. But suppose amendments of the kind foreshadowed by the Prohibition Amendment with deep cultural impact, were to be adopted? Would not fairness require the working out of some method of participation? It seems to me that this is so. But how are we to implement this principle by a suitable institutional framework? A really permanent solution in this instance calls for constitutional amendment, since the amending procedure is regulated in the Constitution. I envisage the insertion of the words "including the Commonwealth of Puerto Rico" at three appropriate points in Article V.[15] But since such an amendment is not too likely to be enacted in the foreseeable future, a compromise might be provided by the Congress. It could agree to an amendment of the Federal Relations Act which would provide that the views of the Puerto Rican people (through their legislature and/or the resident commissioner) shall be ascertained before enacting an amending proposal. If the verdict of Puerto Rico on such a proposal is negative, then a clause would be inserted into it, excluding its application to Puerto Rico, as an associated free commonwealth. It is evident, however, that this sort of arrangement would give Puerto Rico an effective veto, as far as future provisions of the Constitution are concerned, and hence an amendment of the kind suggested would seem decidedly preferable.

A related question is that of amendments of the Puerto Rican constitution itself. It has been argued that such amendments are not subject to congressional control [16] and it is quite possible that this view will prevail. But since the Puerto Rican constitution itself (at congressional insistence) contains an article which subjects revisions of the constitution to the requirement that they be "consistent with the resolution enacted by Congress," and since that resolution demanded alterations of the constitution,[17] it would be desirable to make it explicit that, just as in the case of state constitutions, constitutional amendments are only limited by the terms of the Federal Relations Act and by the Constitution of the United States. What this would specifically mean is that the Puerto Ricans could, e.g., incorporate into their constitution such parts of the Universal Declaration of Human Rights as they considered desirable. Since failure to provide for this freedom served as a basis for some of the most effective opposition in the United Nations to recognizing that Puerto Rico is self-governing, the removal of this blemish would also serve to strengthen the international standing of the permanent solution.[18]

In conclusion, I should like to state that the permanent

status of a free and associated commonwealth, as here outlined, is entirely compatible with American constitutional traditions. It is a novel, indeed a unique concept, but in no sense contrary to these traditions; for it is in line with the basic philosophy of American constitutionalism and federalism.[19] Indeed, it may in some ways be said to be a peculiarly American solution to the problem of how to end colonialism and transform it into a free democratic association. In so far as that turns out to be the case, such a permanent status as an associated state may have world significance. There is little doubt that it has very great importance for the Puerto Rican and the American people. It has been argued by some that this relationship is a complex and difficult one—too difficult to be considered a permanent arrangement. But the history of political institutions is full of illustrations of the enduring strength of complex arrangements. A realistic compromise, taking into account the relevant facts of the community structure, possesses enduring strength, while simpler and more radical solutions fail, because they are the products of the arbitrary will of impatient men. May it not be said that the entire history of democratic constitutionalism is one of developing more complex and yet more adequate institutions, in lieu of the "simple" rule of one man or a small ruling class? Be that as it may, the foregoing sketch of a permanent solution to the problem of Puerto Rico's place within the framework of American government has, it is hoped, shown that it can be done. It may take twenty-five years to work it out, but the present inadequate arrangements may yet be the stepping stone to a genuinely democratic and wholly self-governing Puerto Rico.

NOTES

1. *Annals,* as cited, p. 145.
2. Gordon Lewis, "Puerto Rico: A Case-study of Change in an Under-

developed Area" in *The Journal of Politics*, XVII (1955), pp. 614 ff. at 631.

3. Governor Muñoz Marín also used 1975 as a target year in discussing economic prospects. See *El Mundo*, January 23, 1958.

4. *Ibid.*, p. 626. If Lewis adds that the "key to Puerto Rico is in Washington," implying that this fact raises a great objection to the commonwealth status, the answer should be that the key to Massachusetts or any other state is also in Washington. The fault is not that the key is in Washington, but that Puerto Rico has no share in shaping the key.

5. See the introduction by Robert McCloskey and myself to *The Declaration of Independence* (1954). Cf. also Carl Becker, *The Declaration of Independence* (1942), for a keen appraisal.

6. By the representatives of the powers opposing the motion of Brazil and others to accept the request of the United States to be excused from making further reports on Puerto Rico, as is required for all non-self-governing territories under the Charter of the UN. Notably the representatives of Guatemala, as well as of India and the Soviet bloc made highly misleading representations, based upon material furnished by the Nationalist and Independentist groups (as stated by themselves). It would be tedious to list all the different charges. Nonetheless, among the more telling arguments is the one mentioned in the text. See for the actual discussions the reports for November 4, 1953, pp. 6/7 and p. 14 esp. (A/C. 4/SR. 349). It is not without interest that all these speakers, following the Soviet lead, assumed that only the achievement of independent statehood and sovereignty could be considered a fulfillment of the idea of full self-government. Still, it was uncomfortable that the Czech UN delegate could remark that "it was obvious that the United States considered the Universal Declaration of Human Rights purely a formal statement and had never any intention of allowing the freely associated State of Puerto Rico to enjoy a full measure of self-government in the social field." (*Ibid.*, 352.) It is evident that this situation needs to be rectified.

7. See Magruder, *op. cit.*, p. 20.

8. The problem was discussed by Governor Muñoz Marín in his Kansas City speech, April 23, 1954, where he left open, however, the question of how it was to be done. There are definite proposals being discussed now.

9. See *Studies in Federalism* (ed. Bowie and Friedrich), esp. ch. II, pp. 79 ff. (written by the author). Cf. ch. XII of the work cited above, Chapter II, note 11.

10. The county agent is an example; other instances are found in the housing field and in social security.

11. Fourth Amendment to the Constitution.

12. See above, ch. II, Perloff, *op. cit.*, note 41 in ch. II, pp. 104 ff. Chapter on "Priorities" does not stress the federal aid aspect, however.

13. Art. VII, sec. 3.

14. Presumably the Supreme Court will have to rule on the applicability of the so-called Insular Cases, for one. Does *Downes v. Bidwell* still apply? I should say, no.

15. Article V would then read as follows: "The Congress, whenever two-thirds of both houses shall deem it necessary, shall propose Amendments to this Constitution, or, on the Application of the Legislatures of two-thirds of the several States, *including the Commonwealth of Puerto Rico,* shall call a Convention for proposing Amendments, which, in either Case, shall be valid to all Intents and Purposes, as Part of this Constitution, when ratified by the Legislatures of three-fourths of the several States, *including the Commonwealth of Puerto Rico,* or by Conventions in three-fourths thereof, *including the Commonwealth of Puerto Rico,* as the one or the other Mode of Ratification may be proposed by the Congress." If this three-time repetition of reference to Puerto Rico be deemed unattractive, an alternative possibility would be to leave the article intact, but add to it a phrase to the effect that for purposes of this article, Puerto Rico shall be treated like a state.

16. See Victor Guiterrez-Franqui and Henry Wells, "The Commonwealth Constitution" in *Annals,* note 11 in ch. I, pp. 40–41, and Pedro Muñoz-Amato, "Congressional Conservatism and the Commonwealth Relationship," *ibid.,* pp. 25–26. The latter says flatly that "the Congress recognized that it is the exclusive right of the Puerto Rican people to amend their own constitution." Guiterrez-Franqui and Henry Wells would build the same proposition on article VII of the Puerto Rican constitution. I am sorry not to be able to share this optimism. When Muñoz-Amato cites the fact that Congress rejected a proposal which would have made *all* amendments subject to prior Congressional approval, he overlooks the

fact that such a rejection did not necessarily imply Congress' rejection of its own right to question a *particular* constitutional amendment. The very fact that Congress insisted upon the insertion of an additional provision into section 3 of this article VII, whereunder it is provided that "any amendment" or "revision" of the constitution shall be consistent with the resolution enacted by the Congress in approving the constitution, with the applicable provisions of the U.S. Constitution, as well as the Federal Relations Act and Public Law 600 shows that the Congress reserved the right to examine any amendment with a view to determining whether it fulfills these conditions or not. I would be happier, if at least the determination of these questions had been left to the courts. But in the absence of any provisions to this effect, it must be assumed that Congress reserved this right to itself. It ought to have transferred all of it to the Puerto Rican people, but there is no use in deceiving oneself in a matter of this kind.

17. See the previous footnote for some of the argument. I might add here that the very fact that Congress saw fit to strike some important provisions from the proposed constitution which embodied basic rights as outlined in the *Universal Declaration of Human Rights* (see above, note 5) is ominous, especially in view of the argument (the deleted section is found in Muñoz-Amato, *op. cit.*, in previous footnote, p. 26) that these sections "were contrary to American ideals of government." Indeed, some Congressmen even asserted that they were "socialistic" or "communistic." This was said and done, notwithstanding the fact that American legislation, both federal and state, has been enacted to give effect to everyone of the principles stated, and such legislation, including the Social Security Act, is of course law in the Commonwealth. If congressmen deleted such a set of principles on the ground that they departed "completely from the whole philosophy of the Bill of Rights of our own Constitution," there is no telling what they might do regarding certain possible amendments on the ground that they violated Art. VII, sec. 3 as amended by them.

18. See Rupert Emerson, "Puerto Rico and American Policy Toward Dependent Areas" *Annals*, pp. 9 ff. for a sane appraisal. Cf. also *ibid.*, pp. 16 ff. "From Colony to Commonwealth" by Antonio Frenos Isern.

19. If it is objected that the key to American federalism is its "dualism," i.e., the direct election of the citizen to state and federal government, the answer should be that the concept of "association" represents a further elaboration of this concept, now at times in fact denied for the United States.

Index